Family Politics and Deception in Northern North America and West-Central Africa: Litigating God's Marriage Intention?

Peter Ateh-Afac Fossungu

Langaa Research & Publishing CIG
Mankon, Bamenda

Publisher
Langaa RPCIG
Langaa Research & Publishing Common Initiative Group
P.O. Box 902 Mankon
Bamenda
North West Region
Cameroon
Langaagrp@gmail.com
www.langaa-rpcig.net

Distributed in and outside N. America by African Books Collective
orders@africanbookscollective.com
www.africanbookscollective.com

ISBN: 9956-792-47-0

DISCLAIMER
All views expressed in this publication are those of the author and do
not necessarily reflect the views of Langaa RPCIG.

Table of Contents

Preface

Largely concerned with Family Politics and Deception in Northern North America and West-Central Africa, this book is intended mostly to provoke and enlighten. *Fossungupalogizing* on whether or not Northern North American courts are able to live up to the standard of 'exclusively saying exactly what the law is' in regard of the apparent war between the mounting same-sex marriage legalization drive and the traditional Western religious conception of marriage as endorsed by America's 1996 *Defense of Marriage Act*, the book also tackles some intriguingly troubling matters emanating from African customary marriages and inheritance, subjects presenting some *oddifacism* of marriage and family very similar at times to those engendered by same-sex marriage in Northern North America. Its underlying preaching is that positive things could often be found even in tragedies; meaning that you should learn to make the best of your troubles instead of letting these haunt you – a goal easily attained by cultivating the habit of looking at the larger picture of things. That even one's "stupid" and non-professional ideas could be learning ground to more people than one ever could have imagined.

Introduction

If your spouse or partner can lie to you about his/her children that he/she had before ever meeting you, on what else would such a person not lie about? And if you are truly the drunkard and abusive person that you are painted as being, would you (after discovering this big lie and several others) still go ahead and seek to ameliorate things for both liar and said children? But that is what this 'drunkard and abusive person' talking to you has endlessly tried to do. I know many people would be wondering here: "What on earth was he thinking doing that?" (Fossungu, 2015a: 55)

This book is largely concerned with Family Politics and Deception in Northern North America and West-Central Africa. Behind it is a "bad news" trip I made to Africa in mid-2014. I will obviously be returning to the said voyage.[1] But what is important here is to acquaint you to the preaching that you could often find things positive even in tragedies or things that most others will consider negative. I am certainly not a cockpit preacher but I guess you easily cultivate this habit when you develop the habit of looking at the larger picture of things. In this way, you are able, for example, to

---

[1] Some of what appears in this Introduction is adapted from author's "Introduction: Finding Positives in Negatives" (March 24, 2015) @ http://www.diasporatalk.com/introduction-finding-positives-in-negatives/. A lot of the material in the book also builds on author's research at the University of Windsor known as the Major Research Paper (MRP) titled "Religion, Same-Sex Marriage, and the Courts in American Politics" that was successfully defended on Tuesday, December 23, 2014 in partial fulfillment of the degree of Master of Arts – Political Science. Dr. Stephen Brooks supervised the said research.

put your troubling past to positive use instead of letting it haunt you. Whether you are a professional or not you must have to appreciate that even your "stupid" and non-professional ideas could be learning ground to a lot of people than you ever could have imagined.

Critical as you may find my viewpoint to be, I do not just intend to point fingers but mostly to provoke and enlighten. The book examines, among others, the manner the courts have grappled with the very problematic issues generated by religion and the struggles for same-sex marriage (SSM) legalization in northern North America (Canada and the United States of America), but notably in the United States. It seeks to *fossungupalogize* with you on whether or not the U.S. 'judicial department' has been able to live up to the standard of 'exclusively saying exactly what the law is' in regard of the apparent war between the mounting same-sex marriage legalization drive and the traditional Western religious conception of marriage as endorsed by the 1996 *Defense of Marriage Act* (DOMA). It also tackles some intriguing issues emanating from African customary marriages and inheritance; subjects that present odd faces of marriage and family very similar at times to those created by SSM in Northern North America (hereinafter NNA) that the courts are called upon to grapple with. The power and influence of the American judge are enormous and could not fail to make a lasting impression on Alexis De Tocqueville who wrote about them in his famous *Democracy in America* in 1833. The issue of SSM seems to have accelerated more than ten-fold the American court's power and influence while paradoxically dragging in a lot of questions on the exercise of such enormous powers by unelected officials.

At this point you certainly are pondering on the connection between the DOMA-SSM issues and Africa, a continent which is well known to lean more on the side of what I would describe as African Customary Marriage (ACM). Your query is legitimate and necessitates our taking off to West-Central Africa. Thanks to the online wizardry of Richard Dwomoh (my Ghanaian colleague at the University of Windsor), I was sitting on Ethiopian Airlines Flight Number 503 on May 6, 2014, en route to Douala (Cameroon) via Addis Ababa (Ethiopia) via encore Malabo (Equatorial Guinea). The Addis Ababa to Douala segment of this eye-opening *waka* was on Flight Number 915 – of course, still on "The New Spirit of Africa" (Ethiopian Airlines' Logo). It is not just this telling Logo that put the voyage on a class of its own like *Christickinology*. Like this Love Science, this trip too was so special for a host of reasons. It was the first time I was going to Africa without the usual hassle-filled stopover in Europe (those who have access to the SobaAmerica Forum would better describe lots of such gruesome experiences, especially in France, to you). It was North America (Toronto's Pearson International Airport) direct to Africa. But it was like most of my other trips made to Mama Africa: with the somewhat exception of the January 2007 voyage.

The 2007 journey was the first I made without a pressing hasty call from home like all the others. In short, it was fairly well planned and meant to get there for marriage purposes. I was going to Cameroon in order to formalize things with the parents and other relations of my Bafut fiancé. But something deliberately refused that the trip be different since the usual emergency call still came as I was half-way. While in Zurich (Switzerland), I called a family member to let him and others pick me up at Douala International Airport at such and such date and time. Inspector Elias Akendung's question was: "So you've already heard about it?" Heard about what? I asked, indicating that I was not calling from Canada but from Switzerland from where I was soon to board the next plane headed for Douala. The puzzling news then came reverberating: Fon David Foncha Fossungu of Nwangong died on the same day (in January 2007) I was leaving Canada! Because of this intervening act, the marriage plans did not go as supposed, and the whole enterprise eventually fell apart in 2008. Was that God's intention?

Whatever the answer that may be advanced, this time in May 2014 (seven years later) I was going not because someone had passed away. I was instead travelling to see my sick mother who had insistently been asking for me to come and "give her water to drink" (a phrase with a lot of traditional signification). I had already learnt something from my father's case. He had also been calling for me to come and see him because he had *something* we needed to discuss, and even advising that if transportation was an issue I should still come and he will take care of that. I kept planning and arranging things here in Northern North America (or NNA) to go and see him during the Christmas period of 2002. But to my greatest shock he was not to be there then. I got the news of his having joined his ancestors on 11 October 2002. Did I still have to then put off going to Africa until December 2002? And would I ever be able to know whatever it was that he wanted to tell me? Therefore, when this 'giving water talk' from my frail mother got registered, procrastination was out of the door. Richard was thus very helpful in quickly setting me up with Ethiopian Airlines, thus excluding my usual reliance on travel agents.

I sat on that long non-stop NNA-Africa flight wondering about so many things. For instance, who will be at the airport in Douala to receive me this time? You may be wondering why I would be wondering. Until then I always did not feel like I had reached Africa when (coming from a very large royal family with many members based in Douala) there was always only Elias Akendung (or maximum two, with wife) that I always met at the airport. This time I had also informed just one family of my arrival. But I felt like the royal that I am on reaching Douala because every Fossungu in Douala (some coming from as far as Debundschazone) that could make it was there. For the first time my home-going voyage was not only completely on an African airline operator but I also got an African Royal Welcome at the airport. There were some *nkems* and chiefs, my daughter and her numerous friends and other siblings, other Bangwa notables in Douala, etc. Notably also, I rode home in Chief Blaise Tendongmo Fosanoh's luxurious RAV-4. To cut it short, the new experiences and other unprecedented information about my double-royal roots garnered from this distinctive voyage (and the next one in July 2014 for the funeral ceremony of my mother) motivated my researching into NNA's own *oddifacism* (or odd faces) of marriage and family alongside Africa's. I am hoping that you will enjoy it and learn from the thought-provoking findings of the family politics and deception research whose NNA segment is highly centred in the courts where litigating over the SSM seems to stiffly question God's idea of having created Eve to be Adam's procreation partner.

Reviewing the themes and literature, chapter 1 also provides a critical assessment of the overriding judicial review/democracy debate, showing that the better view is that judicial review is not "undemocratic" simply because it sometimes replaces the decisions of a representative assembly with the judgment of nine, non-elected judges; a position that enormously helps in understanding the rest of the book, including its general findings as enumerated in the concluding chapter.

Using the 1967 interracial marriage prohibition case of *Loving v. Virginia*, the second chapter investigates the issue whether or not God discriminates; and critically discusses some of the implications of the *Loving* case while also examining the SSM cases coming on the heels of the *Loving* decision: beginning with Minnesota's *Baker v. Nelson* in 1971 and moving up to Hawaii's *Baehr v. Lewin* in 1993, which is the first case to rule in favour of SSM, although a constitutional amendment in the state overturned the decision.

Chapters 3 and 4 take us out of the court arena by studying deception and the political economy of deaths, births and marriages in a northern North American West-Central African family in Montreal known as the Cameroon Goodwill Association of Montreal (CGAM). Chapter 3 focuses on analyzing the strategies for coping with deaths within and relating to the CGAM family, as well as the *sociopackist* rules for financial assistance to members. Chapter 4 then continues the vexing story, hinging on births and marriages social packages and the CGAM's general financial management; also tackling some intriguing issues emanating from African customary marriages and inheritance – subjects that present some odd faces of marriage that are very similar to those created by SSM in NNA that the courts are required to grapple with.

We are thus back in the courts in chapter 5 which devotes itself to studying the revolutionary decisions of 2003

(*Goodridge v. Massachusetts Department of Health* and *Lawrence v. Texas*) and of 2013 (*Hollingsworth v. Perry* and *Windsor v. United States*). In 2003 while *Lawrence* decriminalized sodomy, *Goodridge* not only recognized the right of same-sex couples to marry but also redefined the centerpiece of marriage to be commitment, not procreation. *Hollingsworth* and *Windsor* both invalidated (respectively) states' sex-discriminating marriage laws (the mini-DOMAs) and certain portions of the 1996 DOMA, thus also reaffirming respect of federal-state domains in the Union. Chapter 6 presents the conclusion and the general findings of the book.

List of Tables

Chapter 1

Reviewing the Themes, Literature, and the Overriding Judicial Review-Democracy Debate

From the day the Pilgrims stepped off the Mayflower, religion has played a prominent role in American public life. The faithful have been vital participants in nearly every major social movement in U.S. history, progressive as well as conservative. Still, the close intertwining of religion and politics in the last 40 years is unusual, especially in the degree of the politicization of religion itself. Indeed, religion's influence on U.S. politics has hit a high-water mark, especially on the right. Yet at the same time, its role in Americans' personal lives is ebbing. As religion and politics have become entangled, many Americans, especially younger ones, have pulled away from religion. And that correlation turns out to be causal, not coincidental (Campbell and Putnam, 2012: 34).

In the numerous attempts to legalize or ban same-sex marriage in the United States, the recognizable "Turning to judicially created rights as a method of restructuring society" (Bogart, 1994: xi) provides the anchor of this book. In the current era of its history, American political institutions (notably the courts) are called on to manage a highly salient conflict between two longstanding cultural groups of Americans: those who embrace religious traditionalism and those who embrace progressive sexual norms (Black, Koopman and Hawkins, 2011: 285). The question firmly posed relates to whether the courts are equipped with the necessary skills and other attributes to be able to resolve disputes between these groups. Just how prepared the U.S. judiciary is to be able or unable to handle the problem could be gleaned from the following quiz.

Who was the most influential American of the founding era of the United States: George Washington, due to his military and political achievements? Thomas Jefferson, for the Declaration of Independence and the acquisition of the Louisiana Purchase? James Madison, for his "writing" of the Constitution and subsequent service in the House of Representatives, as Secretary of State, and President? Or might it be John Marshall, who served as Chief Justice of the U.S. Supreme Court for 34 years, longer than any other Chief Justice, and whose ground-breaking decisions still affect the lives of every American? It is safe to say that as Madison was the "father" of the Constitution and Washington the "father of the powers of the Presidency," Marshall was the "father of the Supreme Court," almost single-handedly clarifying its powers [*How the Court Became Supreme*].

The Power and Influence of the American Judge

The power and influence of the American judge, as earlier noted, could not fail to make a lasting impression on Alexis De Tocqueville who wrote in his famous 1833 book that,

What a foreigner has the greatest difficulty in understanding in the United States, is the state of the judiciary. There is hardly any political controversy wherein he does not hear the authority of judges invoked;

and he naturally concludes that in the United States, the judge is a powerful figure. However, when he proceeds to examine the constitution of the courts, he does not find there, at first inspection, anything other than the usual judicial power. It appears to him therefore, that judges never become involved in political questions other than by the purest chance; but this same chance seems to occur every day (cited in Radamaker, 1988: 29).

The issue of SSM seems to have enormously accelerated the everyday occurrence of that chance; also aggravating the problem of writing about same-sex marriage, which "is that the topic is fluid and there are important changes almost daily" (Crehan, 2013: 9). It is thus doubtless that SSM is now one of the most litigated issues in modern America; being a phenomenon that is now scathingly regarded as the quintessential "values" issue in American politics. Numerous commentators have portrayed that leading up to the 2004 presidential election several states banned SSM, with gay marriage ban referenda credited with increasing voting turnout in some conservative states. The SSM literature is very large, especially since the 2003 cart-over-turning verdicts of *Goodridge v. Massachusetts Department of Health* and *Lawrence v. Texas*. This book draws heavily on a few of them.

First, there is the three-state comparative study of the SSM issue that is quite "important for what it reveals about law, politics and social movements in the United States" (Crehan, 2013: 10). Next is the study "comparing the Canadian and American experiences in the lesbian and gay rights areas" in order to discover why public policy in two similar and neighbouring states

3

would assume such divergent routes (Smith, 2005: 227). Not to be left out from mention are the equally stimulating analyses on "The Catholic Church's Response to the Massachusetts Gay Marriage Decision" (Cunningham, 2005) and on "Litigating Same-Sex Marriage: Might the Courts Actually be the Bastions of Rationality?" (Gerstmann, 2005)

Although the issue of marriage equality is the same across the United States, some critics like Miriam Smith have found out that it is not nearly as widespread as it is in Canada. What could be responsible for Canada's handling of the issue differently? Some think it may have to do with the Canadian Charter's express clothing of the courts with the power to review all that the politicians are doing. As Bogart (1994: ix-x) indicates, "The Charter equips courts to review all sorts of issues concerning the workings of government, including actually striking down legislation passed by the politicians." Chief Justice John Marshall in *Marbury v. Madison* (1803) made it very clear that "It is emphatically the province and duty of the judicial department to say what the law is. Those who apply the rule to particular cases, must of necessity expound and interpret that rule. If two laws conflict with each other, the courts must decide on the operation of each" (*How the Court Became Supreme*).

Legal jargon calls this 'the power of judicial review' (see Morton, 1992: chapters 10-12; Cappellatti, 1971; and Dimond, 1989). Nikolai G. Wenzel offers us a recent study that dutifully examines the concept of constitutional review by studying three competing systems: the American/Marshall system of judicial review; the Commonwealth/Westminster model of parliamentary sovereignty; and the Kelsen compromise between the two. He assesses each system's strengths and weaknesses, as constitutional framers navigate the treacherous waters between the Scylla of parliamentary tyranny and Charybdis of *gouvernement des juges*; and concludes in the end that neither extreme is perfect, but lessons are drawn from each of the three models (Wenzel, 2013). This fact has probably led some commentators to the declaration that "My response to our national troubles is to enhance debate about a particular aspect of it: the role of the courts. Strong clashes – with wide participation – about the courts' function in Canada will not undermine that institution but rather treat it in a way similar to any of the institutions of government in this country" (Bogart, 1994: ix). While it globally studies Family Politics and Deception, this book, as previously noted, essentially seeks to examine and assess how American political institutions (notably the courts) have managed a highly prominent conflict between what some experts have described as those Americans who embrace progressive sexual norms and those who embrace religious traditionalism.

Judicial Review and the Power of Religion in America

Judicial review on the SSM issue involves the religion clauses of the First Amendment and the Fourteenth Amendment, including its Equal Protection Clause. Religion has always been, and will continue to be a very powerful force in politics and the risks of its combination with political power obviously led to the idea of the requirement of state-church separation. This idea is best exemplified by the United States.[1] The First Amendment to the U.S. Constitution

---

[1] For further discussion of separation of church and state in America, see Campbell and Putnam, 2012; Black, Koopman and Hawkins,

provides that "Congress shall make no law respecting an establishment of religion, or prohibiting the free exercise thereof." The first part of this provision is known as the Establishment Clause, and the second part is called the Free Exercise Clause. Chief Justice Burger in *Lemon v. Kurtzman* explained that the three main evils against which the Establishment Clause was intended to afford protection are "sponsorship, financial support, and active involvement of the sovereign in religious activities."[2] The Fourteenth Amendment reads:

2011; and Mark Douglas McGarvie, *One Nation Under Law: America's Early National Struggles to Separate Church and State* (Ph.D. Dissertation, Department of History, Indiana University, 2000). For contrary arguments that show the breakdown of the 'wall of separation', see Keith Gunnar Bentele, Rebecca Sager, Sarah A. Soule, and Gary Adler, Jr., "Breaking Down the Wall between Church and State: State Adoption of Religious Inclusion Legislation, 1995–2009" 56(3) *Journal of Church and State* (2014), 503-533. Greenhouse also thinks the separation might have been lost in transition while John Witte, Jr. opines that there is even no wall between the two institutions. See, respectively, Carol J. Greenhouse, "Separation of Church and State in the United States: Lost in Transition?" 13(2) *Indiana Journal of Global Legal Studies* (2006), 493-502; and John Witte, Jr., "Separation of Church and State: There Is No 'Wall'" (March 2, 2005) @ http://cslr.law.emory.edu/publications/publication/title/separation-of-church-and-state-there-is-no-wall/.

2 403 U.S. 602 (1971), citing *Walz v. Tax Commission*, 397 U.S. 664 (1970). The American founders certainly could not help not "Think[ing] of medieval popes waging the Crusades — raising armies, sacking cities and conquering territory — in the name of Jesus Christ. Or prelates torturing apostates and heretics during the Inquisition. Or Pope Pius V expelling Jews from the Papal States in 1569. Or Pope Pius XI signing the Reichskonkordat with Hitler, which, in return for winning a measure of freedom for German Catholics under the Nazis, assured silence from the Holy See over the forced sterilization of 400,000 people and then only the faintest of objections to the Holocaust. Or more recently, bishops and other church officials concealing widespread and repeated child sexual abuse by priests" (Linker, 2015).

All persons born or naturalized in the United States and subject to the jurisdiction thereof, are citizens of the United States and of the State wherein they reside. No State shall make or enforce any law which shall abridge the privileges or immunities of citizens of the United States; nor shall any State deprive any person of life, liberty, or property, without due process of law; nor deny to any person within its jurisdiction the equal protection of the laws.

Although the First Amendment only refers to Congress, the U.S. Supreme Court has held that the Fourteenth Amendment makes the Free Exercise and Establishment Clauses also binding on states.[3] In *Cantwell v. Connecticut*, Justice Roberts stated that "We hold that the statute, as construed and applied to the appellants, deprives them of their liberty without due process of law in contravention of the Fourteenth Amendment. The fundamental concept of liberty embodied in that Amendment embraces the liberties guaranteed by the First Amendment" (Black, Koopman and Hawkins, 2011: 333). Since that incorporation, an extensive body of law has incredibly developed in the United States around both the Establishment Clause and the Free Exercise Clause.[4] As the experts tell us, to determine whether an action of the federal or state government infringes upon a

---

[3] See, respectively, *Cantwell v. Connecticut*, 310 U.S. 296, 60 S. Ct. 900, 84 L. Ed. 1213 [1940], and *Everson v. Board of Education*, 330 U.S. 1, 67 S. Ct. 504, 91 L. Ed. 711 [1947].

[4] Some examples of the Establishment Clause are *Cantwell* (already seen); *Sherbert v. Verner* 374 U.S. 398 (1963); and *Employment Division v. Smith* 494 U.S. 872 (1990). Examples of the Free Exercise Clause are *Kurtzman* (already seen); *Zelman v. Simmons-Harris* 536 U.S. 639 (2002); and *Locke v. Davey* 540 U.S. 712 (2004).

person's right to freedom of religion, the court must decide what qualifies as religion or religious activities for purposes of the First Amendment – knowing, as we should, that religion has three dimensions: religious belief, religious belonging, and religious behaviour (see Smidt, 2011: 106-112).

It is as if they were addressing the question, 'Religious Tensions – Friend or Foe?' posed by Benson and Williams (2011: 77-78), that Robert Putnam and David Campbell argue that American religion has experienced two countervailing transformations of polarization and pluralism over the last fifty years. Polarization refers to the emergence of a new religious fault line in American society. Left on its own, they theorize, such a fault line could split open and tear the nation apart. The existence of pluralism, however, is precisely why the fault line has not become a gaping chasm (Putnam and Campbell, 2012: 5).[5] They are obviously referring to what is now popularly known as the 'God Gap' in American politics. As Smidt (2011: 112-113) explains it, the God gap refers to the tendency for the more religious observant to vote Republican and the less observant to vote Democratic. Patrikios (2008) has attempted to somewhat disentangle this thesis though.

As Putnam and Campbell see it, religious pluralism in the United States has not been accompanied by religious segregation – either literally or even metaphorically. On the contrary, they say, rather than cocooning in isolated religious communities, Americans have become increasingly likely to work with, live alongside, and marry people of other religions

---

[5] This argument is almost like the one from Bogart (1994: x) claiming that Canada's "lack of identity is a virtue for it is the basis upon which our aptitude for compromise and moderation (even now being sorely tested) rests."

– or people with no religion – different from theirs. There is thus harmony in America because it is difficult to demonize the religion, or lack of religion, of people you know and, especially those you love. These writers have then concluded that interreligious relationships are so common that most Americans probably pay them little mind, and consider them unremarkable (Putnam and Campbell, 2012: 5-6). Such a theory (as the discussion in chapter 2 would also fortify) may be true to the extent that we are here talking about "our Christian heritage" (Irons, 2011: 329), since it is well known that Christians tend to disregard anything that is not akin to what they know; with plenty of evidence portraying how many of them "had shown limited interest in non-Christian religions and cultures" (Tweed, 1992: 441).

Tweed's view is supported not only by colonialism (see Fossungu, 2013a: chapter 4; Yancy, 2015) and the theory that "Liars just don't think straight, they always *forget* some important details that then hit back like a boomerang" (Fossungu, 2015a: 53, original emphasis). It thus gets propped up as well by the inter-Christian religious Blaine Amendment that sought "to identify the United States as a Christian Protestant nation, which had begun during the Civil War, was revived with the efforts of Supreme Court Justice William Strong and the National Reform Association" (Buckley, 2011: 322; also Yancy, 2015). The Blaine Amendment was simply based on "partisan and anti-Catholic roots" meant "to buttress a pre-existing Protestant culture in schools and other public institutions and weaken potential competitors, particularly Catholic schools" (Black, Koopman and Hawkins, 2011: 312). The Same-Sex Marriage imbroglio has thrust this vexed problem to the foreground.

Massachusetts Bay Colony Governor John Winthrop in 1630 once imagined religion to be a positive, unifying social force in America. Today, however, the reality is that religion has become a source of conflict. Religion may not always be a source of political conflict but it can be, especially in a pluralistic society. When this conflict occurs, cultures compete for legitimacy in the public space and political institutions must provide resolution (Oldmixon, 2011: 285). Courts certainly form part of the political institutions that provide resolution, doing so through litigation, notwithstanding that such "[c]onstitutional restraints on government are tricky and evanescent; government failure (a lapse into anarchy or leviathan) has historically been the norm, and constitutional success an infrequent exception" (Wenzel, 2013: 591). To one Canadian critic, litigation before the courts is not in itself the issue. He sees litigation as obviously performing an important function in resolving disputes that occur in society, ranging from breach of contracts to suit for damages for defective goods to dissolving marriages and other kinds of domestic arrangements and, in the case of criminal law, dealing with questions of guilt. His conclusion is that there should be little or no controversy in this context over resolution of disputes by tribunals created by the legislatures and subject to their control (Bogart, 1994: ix).

In a 2005 study on "Litigating Same-sex Marriage", Gerstmann, an American political scientist of Loyola Marymount University wondered if 'the Courts Might Actually Be Bastions of Rationality'. Evan Gerstmann could be right in his apprehension since litigation on the same-sex marriage topic is of enormous concern. According to certain experts, some of these topics involve complex and difficult social and political questions. The disputes in this category are many and varied but the commonly cited thorny issues include abortion and other questions focused on the situation of women, homosexuality, the protection of minorities, issues concerning the environment, education, and the control of crime (Bogart, 1994: ix). Historically, we are told, most of these issues that have landed in the courts have arisen in two areas, namely, constitutional litigation and administrative questions. The first involves the respective powers of the central and regional governments – known as federalism litigation – while the second touches on the workings of the administrative state. More recently in Canada such issues have come to the foreground because of the Charter of Rights and Freedoms, not leaving out the impact of its predecessor – the Bill of Rights (Bogart, 1994: ix). This discussion will continue with: (1) a look at the arguments for and against judicial review and, (2) some means for limiting judicial review.

Pros and Cons of Judicial Review: Majority Rule or Minority Domination?

The issue of whether judicial review derogates from majority rule to become minority domination could be converted this other query: What if the United States Supreme Court did not have the power to review laws or executive decisions, overturning those that are unconstitutional? How different might life be in the United States? Until 1803 it was not a foregone conclusion that the Supreme Court of the United States would have that power, despite the fact that judicial review had its origins in early seventeen-century England and had been asserted by James Otis in the period leading up to the American Revolution

[*How the Court Became Supreme*]. A relatively minor lawsuit, we are told, led to one of the most important Supreme Court decisions in American history, *Marbury v. Madison,* laying the foundation for the Court's ability to render its decisions about laws and actions. In *Marbury*, the Supreme Court claimed the power to review acts of Congress and the president and deem them unconstitutional, establishing the American practice of judicial review. Through the decision of Chief Justice John Marshall, then, the court assumed the powers that have enabled it to play such a vital role in American life [*How the Court Became Supreme*].

As already obvious, there has been a lot of contention over the role of judicial review in a democracy, turning especially on the legitimacy of unelected judges disrupting or blocking altogether public policy choices made by elected legislators. We need to briefly emphasize here that the better view would seem to be that judicial review is not "undemocratic" simply because it sometimes replaces the decisions of a representative assembly with the judgment of nine, non-elected judges. In many instances, as the critics have further indicated, "the principles that the court intervenes to protect – freedom of political speech and press, freedom of association and thought – are indispensable to the very process that constitute liberal democracy" (Morton, 1993: 460).[6] The edited volume, *Law, Politics and the Judicial Process in Canada* attempts to reconcile judicial review and constitutional democracy (see Morton, 1993: chapter 13) through answering the following question: What special

---

[6] For further discussion of the judicial review, see Maduna (1989: 78-81). Dimond (1989: 5-11) furnishes an extensive analysis of how alternative theories (interpretivism, noninterpretivism) of judicial review wrestle with the dilemma of judicial choice in a democracy. See also Commager (1958: chapter 2).

competence do judges have that legislators would lack? (Morton, 1993: 459) It is thought that, unlike the other two branches, courts are "purposely distanced from the fray, to guard society's fundamental institutions and to protect its organizing ethical principles. Judicial review offers this potential" (Morton, 1993: 460). This theory is important, especially as "[t]he interplay between judicial decisions and politics is complex" (Gerstmann, 2005: 219).

Judicial review and federalism are grounded in the separation of powers and this conversation cannot be complete without also examining the heated controversy over the overrule clause meant to check judicial review in a democracy. W.A. Bogart thinks that no matter the other weaknesses that may be found in his important book on the issue, the "book will totally fail if it does not persuade the reader that we need more rousing arguments about the role for judges in Canada so that we can consciously and with deliberation determine how this largely unexamined form of power ought to be exercised" (Bogart, 1994: x). As contentious as it is, the expressed existence of judicial review in the Canadian framework has been vigorously defended, with several authors maintaining that the Canadian experience under federalism has clearly shown that politics is alive in the country; that is, political initiatives are vital and political mobilization makes an important contribution to the well-being of society even when courts have the authority to protect constitutional values (Whyte, 1992: 472). This claim may be seen in Toronto where George Hislop (a prominent gay activist, speaking after winning same-sex survivor benefits under the *Canada Pension Plan* in November 2004) declared that "I was very confident... we would win. I always knew that Canadians really are interested in fair play. I think that the court has borne that out. We haven't won all the battles, but we're getting there inch by inch." (Cited in Smith, 2005: 225, omission is original).

In also weighing in on the issue, former Canadian Supreme Court Chief Justice Brian Dickson has argued that a country's Supreme Court has the final word on what the Constitution means (Dickson, 1992). Perhaps he had been reading literally what Chief Justice John Marshall stated in the *Marbury* case:

> Those then who controvert the principle that the constitution is to be considered, in court, as a paramount law, are reduced to the necessity of maintaining that the courts must close their eyes on the constitution, and see only the law.
>
> This doctrine would subvert the very foundation of all written constitutions. It would declare that an act which, according to the principles and theory of our government, is entirely void, is yet, in practice, completely obligatory. It would declare that if the legislature shall do what is expressly forbidden, such act, notwithstanding the express prohibition, is in reality effectual. It would be giving to the legislature a practical and real omnipotence, with the same breath which professes to restrict their powers within narrow limits. It is prescribing limits, and declaring that those limits may be passed at pleasure (*How the Court Became Supreme*).

Some Canadian writers have advanced similar arguments in the context of the Charter's notwithstanding clause, Section 33. John D. Whyte states, "It seems perverse to advocate the retention of a provision which is most likely to be used to preclude judicial intervention when that process has its strongest moral claim, and when the radically dispossessed will have no route for salvation other than appealing to courts to intervene on behalf of the Charter values of liberty, equality and due process" (Whyte, 1992: 473-74). The conclusion of the notwithstanding clause's critics is that Canada's constitutional arrangements do not create a logical or principled argument for legislative override of the Charter of Rights (Whyte, 1992: 472). There is a lot of support to Whyte's thesis here, coming from Chief Justice Marshall himself in *Marbury:* "If an act of the Legislature repugnant to the Constitution is void, does it, notwithstanding its invalidity, bind the Courts and oblige them to give it effect? Or, in other words, though it be not law, does it constitute a rule as operative as if it was a law? This would be to overthrow in fact what was established in theory, and would seem, at first view, an absurdity too gross to be insisted on" [*How the Court Became Supreme*].

Some researchers have discovered that some of the greatest challenges to the override clause in Canada,

> come from those who have been historically marginalized: women; gays and lesbians; visible, linguistic and cultural minorities; Amerindians; and the disabled. Significantly, many from these groups are among those who also have the highest expectations concerning the capacity of litigation to effect a reordering of this society. Many of these voices contend that since the existing structures of power and (particularly the political process) have been indifferent at best and even hostile to the interests represented by these challengers, they ought to turn to litigation and harness principle and rationality to

effect the recognition of rights that dulled legislatures and unresponsive bureaucracies have long denied them. Turning to judicially created rights as a method of restructuring society also has the potential to draw us closer to the United States (Bogart, 1994: xi).

Whether or not Canada is drawn closer to the U.S. has nothing to do with those demanding their rights. The primary reason given by those who advocate the elimination of the override clause relates to the fact that the concern that produced the political demand for entrenched rights cannot and should not be defined by the legislative power granted by section 33. The reason, as Whyte argues, is that "political authority will, at some point, be exercised oppressively; that is, it will be exercised to impose very serious burdens on groups of people when there is no rational justification for doing so" (Whyte, 1992: 472). The debate on the American side of the border leans toward the position that the courts should be activists, and that,

> Political representatives should make their moral reasons explicit whenever they legislate, and, in particular, whenever they amend the fundamental law of the nation. The inability or refusal of lawmakers to express the principles underlying their proposals inhibits the sort of deliberation that democratic politics should promote. By legislating on matters of which they lack "articulate knowledge," elected officials risk enshrining popular prejudices into the law (Liu and Sherrill, 2005: 213).

In the particular case of the Federal Marriage Amendment (FMA), the failure of "articulate knowledge" goes hand in hand with a failure of basic fairness. The grounds on which the proponents of the FMA object to gay marriage seem to furnish even more powerful reasons to legislate against heterosexual divorce (Liu and Sherrill, 2005: 213). In addition, unlike the public, legislators, and executive officials, the critics think courts are obliged to actually consider and respond to facts and arguments presented by the gay and lesbian advocates. Furthermore, courts must publicly set out the reasons for their decisions in writing. As a result, the courts should be considered as the bastions of rationality in dealing with same-sex marriage, as compared to other governmental actors (Gerstmann, 2005: 217). Critics of a legislative override in matters of rights note also that "the impetus for the notion that gay people might want and deserve the right to marriages recognized by the state has come almost entirely from the courts—and the handfuls of gay and lesbian plaintiffs (and their lawyers) who have determinedly made their way through the system to achieve unexpected legal victories" (Egan and Sherrill, 2005: 229). Those gains have accentuated the drive from traditionalists/conservatives to limit the courts' activism.

Methods for Reviewing or Limiting Judicial Review

Peter H. Russell agrees with Whyte "that a liberal democracy requires checks and balances and that judicial review based on a constitutional bill of rights is not inherently undemocratic" (Russell, 1992: 485). But where he differs from Whyte is on the democratic principle of how best to enhance and develop our capacity for democratic citizenship (Russell, 1992: 485). Contrary to Chief Justice Dickson's declaration that the American Supreme Court has had "the final word" on constitutional disputes, the history of that country is sprinkled with Supreme Court decisions that have been reversed. Accomplishing this reversal, according to some experts, has been through various means including constitutional amendment, withdrawal of appellate jurisdiction, statutory reversal (that is, new legislation), court-packing and even outright defiance (Morton, 1993: 461). Morton is right about these means as being "a form of legislative review of judicial review" (Morton, 1993: 461). Some of these methods have to be surveyed further, beginning with outright defiance.

Outright Defiance: Many people believe that judges pursue their own policy preferences, and there is widespread disagreement about whether courts can or should rule for same-sex marriage rights given their institutional limitations, their counter-majoritarian role, and the possibility of violent backlash, among other reasons (Gerstmann, 2005: 217). John Marshall who was instrumental in establishing the power of judicial review was not oblivious of this plain fact. In brief, *Marbury v. Madison* arose in the context of the political infighting between the outgoing Adams and incoming Jefferson administrations, particularly in regard to the federal judiciary. At the conclusion of Adams' administration he appointed Federalists (who favoured a strong central government) to many federal judicial positions in order to perpetuate his party's influence in the government. As soon as Jefferson's new administration took office, it repealed a law that had created many of these new judgeships, including that of Marbury, who subsequently sued Secretary of State Madison to deliver the commission that would allow him to assume his job. Marshall faced a dilemma. If the Court asserted its power and ruled that Madison had to give

Marbury his commission, Jefferson was likely to instruct Madison to ignore the ruling, thereby showing the weakness of the court (*How the Court Became Supreme*).

That would be outright defiance that the court didn't need, especially not at that time. Marshall's decision, therefore, offered something to everyone, including the court itself: it said that Marbury had a right to his appointment as the Justice of Peace; chastised Jefferson (the president) for not having given it to him; explained that Marbury had a right to try to reclaim what was offered to him; and then concluded with an explanation of why the Supreme Court could not provide a remedy. The Judiciary Act of 1789, which had granted the Supreme Court the power to issue orders (by way of mandamus) to members of the government, was unconstitutional because it expanded the Court's role beyond what was permitted by the Constitution. As a result, the Court could not act on Marbury's behalf. Very creative, isn't it? This case is also significant because for the first time, the Supreme Court declared an act of Congress unconstitutional as being contrary to the Constitution. This decision was the foundation for the Supreme Court's power of "judicial review," the power by which the Court could determine the constitutionality of laws passed by Congress [*How the Court Became Supreme*].

Court-Packing and Statutory Reversal: Quite apart from the situation that led up to *Marbury*, other examples to substantiate court-packing are not hard to give; notably, President Franklin Delano Roosevelt's attempts to pack the American Supreme Court when it frustrated his New Deal Economic Recovery Programs.[7] Those who defend legislative

---

[7] For further analysis of it, see Kenneth M. Holland, "The Courts in the United States" in Jerold L. Waltman and Kenneth M. Holland (eds.)

reversal of court rulings argue that "elected officials have the better claims than courts to define and rank human rights as well as to make other important decisions about public policy" (Smiley, 1992: 462; also 464). This argument is certainly about the qualifications of members of the legal community (most of who are too positivistic and 'mechanical') to validly speak for a pluralistic society (see Bogart, 1994). Another expert brings out both the negative and positive parts of this argument home by stating that judges "are not immune from political infection...as virtually every member knows. Indeed, bar associations necessarily involve 'politics' upon two separate and distinct levels: A high percentage of the active members who become officers and committee chairmen are also active in national political parties, and do not entirely leave their partisan predilections at the door when they engage in bar association activities..." (Golomb, 1973: 76). The search for the ideal in matters involving rights and morality is terribly elusive and surely impossible. We are left with the inevitability of conflict over both what should be done and who, ultimately, should decide. All these debates in NNA on Judicial Review and the Overrule Clause are essential to understanding the court cases that follow. They are all decisions of courts that construe the legislatures' acts to an extent seemingly at odds with those legislatures' intentions most of the time – the *Loving* case from the 'race-purity' state of Virginia being typical.

The Political Role of Law Courts in Modern Democracies (New York: St. Martin's Press, 1988), 6-30 at 27; and Harvard Law Review Editorial Board, "Round and Round the Bramble Bush: From Legal Realism to Critical Legal Scholarship" 95 *Harvard Law Review* (1982), 1669 at 1674-76. See also Thomas Jefferson's tireless insistence that the executive also has the right (like the Courts and Senate) to pass upon the constitutionality of the acts of the other branches, as outlined in Commager (1958: chapter 2).

Chapter 2

God And Continentalization Politics: From Virginia To Hawaii On The Same-Sex Marriage Highway To Nowhere?

Ask a devout, theologically literate Roman Catholic to describe the institution of the church, and you're likely to be told that it was founded by Jesus Christ at the moment he gave his disciple Peter the "keys to the kingdom of heaven" and vowed that "whatever you bind on earth will be bound in heaven." This made Peter the head of the [U]niversal [C]hurch, empowered to administer the sacraments, spread the Gospel, save souls and forgive sins until Christ's return, as well as to pronounce with infallible authority on matters of Christian faith and morals. Christ also promised Peter that "the gates of hell shall not prevail" against the church — meaning that no matter how corrupt the institution might appear at any given moment of history, it will never be so consumed by evil that it ceases to be capable of fulfilling its God-appointed tasks (Linker, 2015).

This chapter traces the background to SSM to the 1967 inter-racial marriage ban case of *Loving v. Virginia* [388 U.S. 1 (1967)]. The first part studies the *Loving* case and some of its implications while the second examines the SSM cases coming on the heels of the *Loving* decision: beginning with Minnesota's *Baker v. Nelson* [191 N.W. 2d 185 (1971)] in 1971 and moving up to Hawaii's *Baehr v. Lewin* [74 Haw. 530, 852 P.2d 44 (1993)] in 1993, which was the first to rule in favour of SSM, although a constitutional amendment in the state overturned the decision.

Virginia Loving *Continentalization* Politics: Does God Discriminate?

I know that Momany loves talking love a lot. It is not surprising since he has *lovundeleared* a lot of the opposite sex. Being an African man, a lot of people already know how we Africans love heterosexual sex to the extent of loving our polygamous form of marriage. As an expert tells us,

> Sex is something many people like very much but few are willing to talk about it openly. Take a group of African men sitting together and drinking their *mbu* [palm wine]. Notice their reaction when a cock (to leave out dogs that seem to last forever) suddenly climbs on a hen for the reproductive routine in plain view. See them all turning and looking away as if those fowls are crazy to be doing what they are doing. Yet, these are people who love the sexual act to an extent of wanting to have as many women as they possibly can. No waiting period when one woman is 'indisposed' (Fossungu, 2015a: 13-14, original emphasis)

While the theory on open discussion of sex would seem not to be wholly valid in relation to one of Momany's siblings of the household (see chapter 3), it is clear that Africans do not even generally imagine what northern North Americans have either legalized (Canada) or are struggling to legalize (USA) – man-on-man and woman-on-woman. *Tuffiakwa!* That is not me speaking here, some Ghanaians are. I am in NNA, no doubt; but I have hardly been to Virginia. So I could not even be talking about any *lovundelearing* encounter there with any lady, let alone a man. Virginia's *Loving* deals with inter-racial marriage although its connection with the *homonista* planet is a direct and historical one.

Some commentators think that the question of where to begin the analysis of the struggle relating to same-sex marriage is difficult since it can easily be argued that getting to the historic place of same-sex marriage rights today has been influenced by the gay rights movement, the women's rights movement, and the civil rights movement (Crehan, 2013: 13). This perspective is shared by a 2005 "brief paired comparison of Canada and the U.S. in order to explore the cross-national variance in public policy in the lesbian and gay rights area" (Smith, 2005: 225). As Miriam Smith has argued, Canada and the United States

> are similar systems in many respects, sharing a common history, language, culture, legal roots, and religious heritage. Both societies have undergone substantial social change since the 1960s. With the rise of the women's movement and the increased participation of women in the labor force, both countries have witnessed important changes in family forms and gender relations. In both cases, the gay liberation and women's movements of the late sixties and early seventies gave rise to the modern lesbian and gay rights movement, focused on securing liberal citizenship rights for lesbian and gay (and, more recently, bisexual and transgender) people (Smith, 2005: 225).

Some observers have nonetheless cautioned against the over aligning of these other movements (like Miriam Smith has wisely avoided doing) with the civil rights one since, "[i]n striking contrast to the African-American civil rights movement, where legal action was often carefully coordinated with political strategy," the battle over gay marriage initially caught gay leaders by surprise; with many of them shunning and discouraging the litigation, believing it to be a certain loser that would lead to backlash (Egan and Sherrill, 2005: 229). Talking about African-American civil rights movement in America and family forms would unavoidably bring to mind race relations, with *Loving v. Virginia* not just surging forward, but also obviously being "the place to begin the analysis of federal constitutional law on the issue of same-sex marriage" (Crehan, 2013: 16). This landmark case was decided on June 12, 1967, with Chief Justice Warren delivering the opinion of the Court. The detailed facts of the case are important to an understanding of not only the ruling's eventual impact on lesbian and gay rights but also of the colourization and monopolization of the continents.

Colourizing and Monopolizing the Continents and *Badifying* (the European) God?

Badifying means "giving a bad name to". But you might not quite understand why European is put in brackets until you begin to realize, first, that the ordinary Christian's view of the Church (that opens this chapter) is quite far from the reality. As Damon Linker continues with his enlightening investigation,

> Ask an informed historian or journalist about the history of the church — especially the Vatican and the papacy — and you are likely to hear a different story. On

this telling, the church from the beginning has been an all-too-human institution that often follows... [the] logic of self-interest, placing the good of its members ahead of those outside it, and the good of those in positions of ecclesiastical power ahead of the good of everyone else. To a greater or lesser extent, this has been true of most institutions throughout history, though it has been a particular problem in the 2,000-year history of the church, with its lack of democratic accountability and deep roots in the corruption-prone political culture of the Italian peninsula. The result has been a tension — and sometimes a blatant contradiction — between the church's exalted claims for itself and its behaviour (Linker, 2015).

Moreover, it could also be visualized from how some non-European people also quickly indulge in always blaming *their* own God at the slightest obstacle. For example, having been refused a visitor visa by the Canadian Embassy in Yaoundé for the second time, Momany's wife wrote to him on November 30, 1998, stating:

.... Dear, so it is certain that we are going to spend our Christmas and [marriage] anniversary apart again? *Our own God* is really prolonging things for us, if you had enough money you could have even come and visited me (us). [But w]hen you come people will start expecting so much from you, especially now that your people keep asking if you have not yet started working. Dear, if one were to take what they say and feel, one will be very disturbed and worried.

What can I tell you again apart from the fact that I miss you so much and really long to see you?…

Your lovely wife, Schola [emphasis supplied].

The *Eugenizationing* Monologue: The Longest Letter Ever Written?

Giving you the long missives (as I have) in this book in their entirety is essential to an easy grasping of both the points and the context in which they were penned. Paraphrasing some of these written communications usually ends up detrimentally taking much wind out of the sails, thus bomb-dropping on a lot of the vigour of the theory or theories these communications are meant to advance or fortify. One of these hypotheses concerns Mrs. Loving who I am certain was not just lovely like Scholastica but also a dedicated and God-fearing wife. I say this because you will see Scholastica herself ceaselessly letter-preaching while still in Cameroon about what she would do on reaching NNA by God's grace. How when she comes to NNA she would do everything, anything, all things, to bring Heaven and Paradise to the family; and precisely to "My Darling Power" who is "a nice husband" "because thinking and remembering you carry a lot of hope of happiness for today and tomorrow." And especially how "My problem now is our kids [because it] is not nice to pass through a certain age without having kids." Very impressive and convincing, you would join me in saying. God too was unquestionably very impressed and *marryfully* worked the miracles for her triumphant 'Coming to America'.

But just get Scholastica's promised Blissful and Harmonious Family Progress, uncensored, in Momany's

26

longest letter ever of October 22, 2001 (two years after her arrival in Canada) to "Dear Eugene", her brother:

I am sorry this letter must come to you as a surprise, being, I think, quite a long time since I wrote to you. Well, the letter itself explains why [there has been] this apparent long silence. One thing that I must emphasize: what I am telling you here is merely for information purposes. There is nothing you can do to change anything. Neither can your dad to whom I should actually be writing this note. Considering his state of health, I have avoided bringing this to his attention but you are the one who can validly represent him in his absence. I'll try to be as short as I possibly can be notwithstanding that a lot of things have been going wrong for quite a long time now with us here.

You can remember the circumstances under and through which Scholastica got here. You can as well remember the struggles and challenges I have gone through since her abrupt arrival here in order to regularize her stay. Having gone through it all until she got her papers, I thought things were then going to be better for us all, but especially for family members back home. But as of this very moment I am writing, things have instead been moving in the wrong direction despite all my attempts at making your sister see that we both have to cooperate, sacrifice certain personal things for now until we can help others that are so much dependent on us. How has Scholastica so far taken this? She has accused me of not wanting to see her succeed in life; that is, that I have gone to school until the end of it and now I don't want her to go to school also.

You remember very well how you told us about your field work in Limbe long in advance and we promised to aid you. But did we? Why not? At the time Scholastica was doing her training in tailoring. She was lucky to have to be paid $200.00/week for doing it. Luckily also, a little afterwards I also got a work permit for ten months. But could I actually make good use of my permit? No. Because everyday Scholastica left her training and connected to university for classes. And remember that it was at the same time that Ngunyi was always sick at the daycare and we had to withdraw her from it. I was at home with her. My suggestion again was that Scholastica put off the classes for the time being, finished training and come home so that I can then work in the evening or night. She was so adamant on continuing with her school, accusing me as usual. Six months of the tailoring training were over and they had to place her in a tailoring job. She refused, saying the job was too strenuous for her. "Then why did you do the training?" No response. She had only been interested in the money given her and her courses at the university. She thereafter started going to school full-time. What could $200.00/week do to keep the family going? Absolutely nothing.

Later on I got a job in the night (11.30 PM. – 7.30 AM) since she finished school that late. Because things were not moving on well financially, I tried also getting something for the day as well. These are all factory jobs, mark you. Nothing to do with my studies. What people call mean jobs. But I am prepared to do all that because I know where we stand and what we have to do to help others back home. I was lucky to get another job that began at 8 AM to 5 PM, The arrangement was that

Scholastica could drop the baby at the daycare before going to school and try to be home before 10.00 PM. I picked her up from there at 5.30 PM. But before I knew it, Scholastica came up with a job that began at 7.00 AM, meaning she had to leave the house at about 6.00 AM. What does that mean? That I should drop the night job. I didn't see anything wrong because I was even trying to do two jobs simply as she was not working. I remained with the day job alone and had to be the one to drop the child at the daycare. This also meant I had to be going late often. I used to connect from the night job to the other one without any problem of lateness. I started having problems at the job. All this [was] for nothing because Scholastica's job actually began at 7.30 AM, not 7.00 AM, as she had said.

But that is not all. Before long (2 months) she left the job and started schooling again full time. And all this she did without us discussing anything because she had initially made it absolutely clear that any arrangement or discussion that did not revolve around her schooling should be forgotten. How come you decided to take up this job that cost me my own jobs only to now abandon it? No answer. How are we going to help Eugene and others as promised? No answer that is convincing and pragmatic: "If I don't study, I can't have a good job that will permit me to help my family." But what about the help they need right away? 'Leave me alone' is the only response I get. And if I persist in trying to make her see the point, the usual sing-song: "You've gone to school until you're now a doctor and you don't want me to progress. I'll progress all the same despite that everyday you're praying for my failure." Yes, you say all that but don't you see what I am doing (odd jobs) with all that education? And what guarantees do you have that you will have your dream job as soon as you finish? And what if by the time you have this dream job there is nobody there for you to help? Why can't you just for one moment stop being so self-centred? Why can't we be hanging on something at least while looking for something better? What will we do when my work permit expires? All this did not ring a bell in her head.

Before long, you were knocking confidently for the aid promised you. Your dad's illness came; mum's illness too was there; etc. When your dad's situation was told us, she turned to me, asking me if I had heard. I said I had. And she asked: "What do you say?" I put the question back to her: "What do you want me to say?" She has since been calling people here and there, saying that I take her family for granted, etc. And she is the one who is very good also at insulting me every now and then how I have neglected my mother and the like. I really do wonder at times if the person I am listening to is actually someone who is right here with me and living the reality of what I am going through. Since October 5, 2001, I have been sitting at home because my work permit expired on that date. Scholastica does not even think about what we are going to do to be able to pay the bills at the end of the month. She seems not to be worried about the rent, feeding, etc. She is only leaving every day and going to school. She doesn't need any work permit to work, or any student authorization to study. She can stay in Canada for as long as she wants, even for life. She can sponsor any of her family members now to come to Canada and also stay as long as he or she wants. I don't have any of these rights. And I am among those (including you all back there as her brothers and sisters, mum, dad) that she can sponsor. BUT to do so, she must show proof of means to support the person(s). Having a regular job for herself is a very important requirement for all this. But how can she sponsor even me who am right here with her when the evidence will all point to the fact that she depends almost entirely on me? As I said earlier, she is not even worried by the fact that I have not been working since October 5. She is not concerned that my application for a new work permit may eventually be refused. She is not even thinking about going out to work until I can again begin to work. All she does think about is her schooling.

Last Saturday (October 29, 2001) she called my sister's house in the USA and talked all kinds of thrash to them about me: How I don't do anything at home, how I treat her so badly, how she has been suffering since she came to Canada, etc. She later handed the phone to me that they on the other end wanted to talk to me. I told her to go to hell with all [what] she was trying to do.

Frankly, I am really sick and tired of being sick and tired. I'm sick and tired of being considered as seeking someone's downfall simply because I try to make the person see reason. I'm sick and tired of having someone always trying to tell me that cooperating means I must always accept his or her views or there is no cooperation. I'm really sick and tired of trying to reason someone that seems to be beyond being reasoned. I'm sick and tired of having an innocent baby girl being used as an instrument of intimidation or blackmail. I am sick and tired of having someone trying to live as a couple in certain instances but as an independent or single person in others. I am sick

31

and tired of being regarded as an obstacle to someone's advancement and, therefore, I think the better thing for me to do will be to get out of being sick and tired and out of the way.

As I have emphasized above, this is solely for information purposes. There is nothing any of you back home can do to alter anything if I have not been able this far to do so right here.

Extend my greetings to everyone and good luck in your undertakings,

Sincerely yours, [signature].

The Lovings' dedication to their own union wasn't shaken by the strong and state-organized negative winds of Virginia.[8] In June, 1958, two residents of Virginia, Mildred Jeter (a Negro woman like Scholastica) and Richard Loving (a white man unlike Power) were married in the District of Columbia pursuant to its laws. Shortly after their marriage, the Lovings returned to Virginia and established their marital abode in Caroline County. At the October Term, 1958, of the Circuit Court of Caroline County, a grand jury issued an indictment charging the Lovings with violating Virginia's ban on interracial marriages. On January 6, 1959, the Lovings pleaded guilty to the charge, and were sentenced to one year in jail; however, the trial judge suspended the sentence for a

---

[8] It is thus well known that "both Schola and Flavie have been the *real things* that have been keeping me so *drunken* that I could not have written a thing while they were in my blood stream and perturbing my head. Else, it is not clear how we are to explicate the fact that, from 1996, I was producing at least one academic journal article every year until 1999 when Schola got to Canada: with my next article thereafter only appearing in 2010" (Fossungu, 2015a: 54, note omitted). What does one make of these women's 'for better, and for worse'?

period of 25 years on the condition that the Lovings leave the State and not return to Virginia together for 25 years. He stated in an opinion that: "Almighty God created the races white, black, yellow, malay and red, and he placed them on separate continents. And, but for the interference with his arrangement, there would be no cause for such marriage. The fact that he separated the races shows that he did not intend for the races to mix." [388 U.S. 1 at 4 (1967)]

Theatrealization: Monopolization and/or Ignorance?

Theatrealization simply describes the *champ d'étude* or theatre of action. Hasn't the great political philosopher John Stuart Mill been quoted by Gerstmann (2005: 217) for once asking, "Was there any domination which did not appear natural to those that possessed it?" Otherwise, first, wouldn't this same race-purity God have sufficiently instructed these white people to remain on their own continents without crossing over to those of the other races and causing trouble (interference) there? Doesn't this very argument (like the Liars-Don't-Think-Straight thesis) completely nullify Europeans' so-called justification for "civilizing" the other races/continents? Answering a question on how North America's "amnesia" contributes to forms of racism directed uniquely toward Native Americans in our present moment and to their continual genocide, Noam Chomsky has this to say:

> The useful myths began early on, and continue to the present. One of the first myths was formally established right after the King of England granted a Charter to the Massachusetts Bay Colony in 1629, declaring that conversion of the Indians to

Christianity is "the principal end of this plantation." The colonists at once created the Great Seal of the Colony, which depicts an Indian holding a spear pointing downward in a sign of peace, with a scroll coming from his mouth pleading with the colonists to "Come over and help us." This may have been the first case of "humanitarian intervention" — and, curiously, it turned out like so many others.

Years later Supreme Court Justice Joseph Story mused about "the wisdom of Providence" that caused the natives to disappear like "the withered leaves of autumn" even though the colonists had "constantly respected" them. Needless to say, the colonists who did not choose "intentional ignorance" knew much better, and the most knowledgeable, like Gen. Henry Knox, the first secretary of war of the United States, described "the utter extirpation of all the Indians in most populous parts of the Union [by means] more destructive to the Indian natives than the conduct of the conquerors of Mexico and Peru (Yancy, 2015).

Second, would the fact that 'Almighty God created' the sexes, male and female, and placed them on *all* the continents not also mean as well that he intended the sexes to mix? If sexes are also not to mix, what then would this particular judge say to homosexuals (one of whom he might even be, by the KKK-DL)? That is, the Ku Klux Klan-Dubious Logic of homosexual in hiding and heterosexual in public as seen in Fossungu (2015a: 97-98). Third, would this judge be unaware that the monumental *Brown v. Board of Education of Topeka* [347 U.S. 483 (1954)] invalidating segregation in public schools, decided 13 years before *Loving*, clearly "gave the needed signal that the promise of the preamble's pledge would not continue to go unheeded"[9]? Let us go into some details relating to some of these queries, with first focus on the theatre of action.

As previously indicated, this book examines the manner in which the courts have wrestled with the very problematic issues generated by religion and the struggles for SSM in NNA, with the United States in the driver seat. This section is meant to situate the playground, with two main issues of Monopolization and of Ignorance aiding in bringing *fosungupalogy* to the whole of NNA – supposedly a place of abode for those that Tocqueville termed "a nation of joiners"[10] for being quick to assert their rights,[11] including the right to marriage and family. Northern North Americans must acquaint themselves with *fossungupalogy* because Andrew L. Sonner is not alone in telling us that "Ignorance Is No Excuse."[12] I am talking about "the science of straightforwardness, necessitating the fearless looking at truth

---

[9] Peter W. Rodino, "Living with the Preamble" 42 *Rutgers Law Review* (1990), 685 at 690.

[10] Wilson A. Head, "The Ideology and Practice of Citizen Participation" in James A. Draper, ed., *Citizen Participation: Canada* (Toronto: New Press, 1971), 14-29 at 15.

[11] Though, paradoxically, Professor Michael Nelson of Vanderbilt University "would bet that for every thousand people in this country [United States] who could list the Bill of Rights and name all nine Supreme Court justices, you would be lucky to find one who could explain the his rights against federal agencies and name the members of even one [of the myriad of] regulatory commission[s]" Michael Nelson, "Bureaucracy: The Biggest Crisis of All" in Charles Peters and Nicholas Lemann (eds.), *Inside the System* 4th ed. (New York: Holt, Rinehart and Winston, 1979), 315-325 at 324.

[12] Andrew L. Sonner, "Ignorance Is No Excuse" 7:2 *Criminal Justice* (Summer 1993) inside cover. Section 75 of Cameroon's Penal Code (1965-67) is to the same effect.

straight in the eye" (Fossungu, 2015b: xi). I may not be an expert on NNA politics generally, but I believe strongly that one does not need to be an expert to understand experts and/or make a point or two to them. All what I think it takes a non-expert to do some of these things is just the audacity not to be bullied or frightened away by the experts' high-sounding formulations. The expertise I *may* lack (which I doubt) but surely not the boldness to talk to the experts and be told that. I invite you therefore to fasten your seat-belts and enjoy this intra- and intercontinental flight as (in the manner of Gabon's Jean Ping[13]) I daringly attempt a reduction of some of the advanced-looking and intimidating conceptions of the states and families concerned to the nothingness that some of them actually are, especially when put through the *fossungupalogistic* litmus paper. Let's then commence welcoming *fossungupalogy* to America with an *expibasketical* racial profiling case and a bit of the globalization chitchat.

An *Expibasketical* Racial Profiling Case and the Globalization Chitchat

Take the first issue first with my lengthy letter of July 31, 2006 to Mr. Brian Rossy (the owner of the company). Containing many points of interest to this discussion of racism in NNA, it was titled "A Complaint Regarding Constant Workplace Harassment and Racial Profiling" and read:

---

[13] See Rekngwese, "The Internet to Liberate Africa" (March 25, 2015) @ http://www.diasporatalk.com/the-internet-to-liberate-africa

Dear Sir: My name is Peter A. Fossungu and I began working for your company on March 6, 2001. I will enumerate just a few instances here to buttress this complaint.

Sometime in 2002 or 2003 (I am not very sure which but Mr. Alfred Weindrich can fill us up on this since he has the exact date on a piece of paper that he intimidated me to sign), I had a misunderstanding with another employee, Mr. George (who is now retired). He went up to Mr. Weindrich, the warehouse manager, who – without even bothering to hear what I also had to say concerning the matter – immediately dressed up a four-day suspension paper and then called for me and threatened me to sign it. I refused to sign, clearly indicating to him that the manner he had handled the issue bears clear witness to the fact that he has some special problems with me that I did not until then know of.

About four months later, I (as a quality inspector) was trying to instruct another employee (from the agency) on how to correctly perform his duties as a distributor. I politely asked him to watch while I corrected his errors in two stores and then asked him to continue in the same manner. But he still piled up glass products on one another too high rather than spreading them evenly on the skid. When I approached him to know why he was doing what he was doing, he barked out: "I HATE WORKING WITH FUCKING BLACK PEOPLE". I took the matter up to Mr. Alfred Weindrich who, instead of sanctioning the employee concerned, told me that I always like to make a big issue out of small things. When, because of the manager's way of handling the issue, some black workers demonstrated their anger, I was again singled out by the manager and threatened with dismissal for, as he put it, "attempting to form a trade union". It took some officials from your Human Resources Department to arrest the escalating situation that ensued.

The year 2005 saw an accentuation in the harassment and racial profiling with the arrival of Mr. Steve Donofsky. It now seems to me that this employee was brought into the scene for the single and sole purpose of harassing me out of your company. The incessant harassment and racial profiling from both Mr. Donofsky and Mr. Weindrich – meant to indirectly drive me away – reached their peak especially in May and June 2005. It culminated in their demotion of me from quality inspector to distributor in July 2005. The reason they gave then was that the inspection department was being closed down for not being productive. But three days after the supposed closure I found that Serge Beaudry, a white guy, was back doing inspection. As soon as I attempted to begin doing inspection, Mr Donofsky (who is always on my heels) began barking at me: "What are you doing?" I responded by telling him to direct his question first to Serge (who was inspecting just nearby) before asking me for an answer. He became hysterical, insisting and threatening, as usual, that I must answer his question. I then told him that he had eyes and did not therefore need my answer. I was summoned to appear in Mr. Weindrich's office where I was reprimanded for questioning his supervisors. When I asked to know why Serge was back inspecting, Mr. Weindrich responded that he had personally authorized him to do so. Why him and not me also? The only answer I got was "That is none of your business".

About four months ago, Mr. Mohamed Faez (another supervisor employed about two years ago) had some misunderstanding with me. As is usual with all of Mr. Alfred Weindrich's supervisors, Mr. Faez went hysterical when I tried to reason with him. He kicked and scattered on the floor most of the boxes on the skid that I was distributing. He was even about using force on my person when some other employees (about five of them) intervened and restrained him. He then went to Alfred and told him a completely different story: that I had scattered all the boxes on the floor, blocking circulation and impeding others from working. Without seeking to know from witnesses at the scene or even hearing what I had to say, Mr. Weindrich made his decision of suspending me and then called for me to say so. He further indicated to me that I was being paid for nothing. Before leaving, I told him that he had better do something to put things right because I particularly hate being paid for nothing.

On 27 July 2006, when Mr. Donofsky harassed me, I went to Mr. Weindrich to request that he instructs the former to desist from further harassment of me because it had reached a point where I was going to do something about it. All I got from Mr. Weindrich was rebuke. No witnesses were required at all. Mr. Weindrich made it clear to me that I could never have a case as far as he is concerned. I then told him that I was very aware of that fact but that he ought to know that he will not be the sole judge in any suit I institute for workplace harassment and racial profiling against Mr. Weindrich, Mr. Donofsky, and Dollarama L.P./S.E.C. jointly and severally. Most of what happened on 27 July 2006 between 11 a.m. and 1 p.m.

could be found in your security camera because the arguments of my having no case and threats of expulsion began in Mr. Weindrich's office and ended in front of the security desk outside.

The next day, on 28 July 2006, Mr. Donofsky carried on his job of harassing me by parking his cart right in the middle of the passageway when he saw me approaching. Because I had adopted (as a better response to his constant harassment) silence and ignorance of his presence, I tried to find a way to pass by without talking to him. The space available was not enough for my skid, which caught his parked cart. He then mockingly took off his eyeglasses and asked if I needed them to see. I nodded. He threw them at me and I caught them. I asked him what he would do if I broke them. I then threw them back at him. He deliberately let them fall to the ground and then said I owed him a hundred and fifty dollars ($150.00). I turned around and was going but he rode his cart and parked it right before me and the electric jigger that I was pulling. Of course, I yelled to him: "Move it!" I had to escape from being caught between the abruptly parked cart and the moving old jigger whose brakes were not as efficient. The jigger lightly hit Mr. Donofsky's cart. He did all the swearing and headed for Mr. Weindrich's office. About five to ten minutes later Mr. Weindrich and Mr. Kamil came to where I was working and asked me to come to the office of the former. In the office and in the presence of Mr. Kamil, Mr. Weindrich asked me to sign a piece of paper. I asked what it was all about and he said it concerned what had just happened between Steve and me. Mr. Kamil was present in the office during this particular instance and witnessed the entire event. Mr.

Kamil could be a key witness, he is beyond the menace that the warehouse employees are subjected to and he could (from his short experience on this day) brief you on the racist and menacing style with which the warehouse is run. For example, it was only when I insisted on having Mr. Donofsky present before I could talk about what had happened that he was brought in. Quite understandably, my version of the story and his were substantially different regarding essential details. Mr. Weindrich (who has never cared to bring in any witnesses whenever I have been involved in any disputation) now – perhaps solely because Mr. Kamil was there – asked Steve to go and look for witnesses. At the end of the whole episode involving witnesses with predictable and influenced testimonies, I still refused to sign the paper that had been prepared before I was brought into the picture. I indicated, as my reason for not signing, that it was a complete farce, being not only prejudicial but also having only racial profiling and intimidation as its base.

I just thought I should keep you informed because I am seriously considering talking to my lawyer for the necessary legal action unless important steps are taken within the company to stop the incessant racial profiling and to make my work environment comfortable and harassment-free.

Yours sincerely,

Peter A. Fossungu

The manner in which the company reacted to this bold complaint is reminiscent of what you hear in the globalization chinwag. John Akokpari (like many others) would argue that globalisation, which has become an undisputed phenomenon in the post-Cold War era, is not new. Rather, it is an acceleration of the process of capital accumulation and exportation to the South, which has been in place since the seventeenth century.[14] However, in the post-Cold War era this process changed qualitatively from its previous character with the emergence of new global institutions such as the World Trade Organisation (WTO) and regimes like the Uruguay Rounds Agreements (URA) which now supervise and regulate trade among nations.[15] These new global institutions include the international financial institutions (IFIs), two of which are "the IMF and the World Bank [which the Mayor of London, Ken Livingstone, says] had killed more people than had Adolf Hitler" (cited in James, 2009: 1).

James goes on to categorize Livingstone's statement as "demonstrat[ing] his lack of either historical sense or responsibility" (James, 2009: 1) but I think James would just be trying to stay true to what Jack Goldsmith has branded as "organized hypocrisy"[16] and Noam Chomsky as "intentional ignorance" (Yancy, 2015). Organized hypocrisy or ignorance, they must be shown the door. Yes. I think we have to start looking at most of these issues straight in the eye to be able

---

[14] See Akokpari, 2001; Niall Ferguson, *The Ascent of Money: A Financial History of the World* (New York: Penguin Books, 2008); and Dani Rodrik, *The Globalization Paradox – Democracy and the Future of the World Economy* (New York: W.W. Norton, 2010).

[15] See Akokpari, 2001; and Anna Lanoszka, *The World Trade Organization: Changing Dynamics in the Global Political Economy* (Boulder: Lynne Rienner Publishing, 2009).

[16] See Snigdha Nahar, "Sovereign Equality Principle in International Law" *Global Politician* (2008) at n.19, available @ http://globalpolitician.com/default.asp?24351-international-law; and James Ferguson, *Global Shadows: Africa in the Neoliberal World Order* (Durham: Duke University Press, 2006) at 25-49.

to see the gross deception that is clothed in some 'new' and 'nice-sounding' concepts which end up just replacing one form of oppression with a more insidious form. The Archbishop of Washington puts it better,

Today, many would have us believe that to present marriage as the union of a man and a woman is "discrimination" and as such should be punished. They would tell us that our rejection of abortion offends their sense of personal liberty and we must change our position if we intend to participate in the works of the common good.

This increasingly loud position implies that freedom extends only to those who share this new "moral code," a redefinition of human life, marriage, sexual activity, and morality. For them, it is not bigotry to challenge Catholic teaching. It only becomes bigotry and discrimination, they say, when Catholics assert our beliefs (Wuerl, 2015).

Anglospheridism and the Ignorant West-Central African Cultural Advisers: Two Diseases or One?

Cardinal Wuerl could be right about this rising and unbecoming 'my way or no way' posture in American politics, both internal and external. And you see this too in the monopolization of North America. Most people talk or write about North America in terms that equate it with Canada and the United States of America. Like American writers claiming to write about 'all religions of the world' (see Tweed, 1992), such 'North America' talkers are either (1) suffering excessively from the disease called *Anglospheridism*[17] or (2) are

[17] "America's macrostrategic environment is chockablock with assets unavailable to any other country. If nothing else, the United States has an often-overlooked and oft-neglected bulwark of allies: the

mere victims of/from the Ignorance-Jammed Continents. That could explain why an expert has implored us to "do add 'ignorant' to the negative, please, before welcoming them to the new ignorance-jammed planets" (Fossungu, 2015a: 82).[18] Yes, mainland North America is composed of three countries, one of which is Mexico that is a party to the NAFTA (North America Free Trade Agreement). The last 'A' can be anything: Accord, Association, or Act. Whatever the 'A' begins does not change NAFTA to anything that excludes Mexico.

Because this particular North American country is Spanish-speaking, there is this unwise or unthinking tendency of bumping it up with Latin America, thus seeking to deprive it of its North American appurtenance. Of course, Mexico is

---

Anglosphere....With a combined population of 420 million, with strategic locations off the continent of Europe (Great Britain), near the intersection of the Indian Ocean and western Pacific sea-lanes (Australia), and in the Attic and adjacent to Greenland's oil and gas (Canada), the Anglosphere, if not abused or ignored, will be a substantial hard-power asset for the United States deep into the twenty-first century. China and Russia enjoy nothing comparable" Robert D. Kaplan and Stephen S. Kaplan, "America Primed" *The National Interest* (March/April, 2011), 42-54 at 44-45.

[18] "Most Moroccans and Algerians in Rossy Inc., for example, would tell you that they are not Africans, but Arabs. This makes me to then wonder if someone could quickly want to find out from them what the hell they are still doing on the continent and also competing in African sports and the like? From this narrative, you can see that they are obviously equating African with the Blackness that they too have come to the continent probably to 'whiten' or civilize with their Islam. At this juncture, I then also realize that those Arabs are not alone since it is also equivalent to some (Western) Europeans behaving as if Turks are not Europeans because of their being Muslims. All that then leads me to the theory that whether those denying the plainest of facts like it or not Turks are Europeans until you can and have successfully cut Turkey off the continent called Europe and taken it, perhaps, to the 'yet to be created' continent called *Moslema* or *Islamagood*" (Fossungu, 2015a: 83-84).

44

Latino (by virtue of its language). But haven't we already monopolized that terminology for South America (Latino America, it is said?) in the same way as the U.S. has monopolized 'American'? (Who thinks of us Canadians when 'American' is ever used?) Or, does South America effectively mean 'south of' America? If that be the case, should North America then not also exclude America itself, leaving us with just the *copyocratic hypocracy* called Canada that is 'north of' America? What a folly of a North American monopolizing disease! I am clearly not a *copyocrat* or a sufferer of any of these diseases. Using 'English-speaking North America' in the title of this book would have done the job. But that would also expose the folly of excluding us Quebecers, a Canadian favourite pastime[19] that is also propped up by the impractical Canadian talk of 'Canada and Quebec'. Hence, my employment of 'Northern North America' to make clear that I am not about to discuss these issues as concerns Mexico, about which I am not vest but about whose continental presence I am not ignorant like the American *likehewasians*. Black Africa itself is not devoid of such ignorant pests.

As for the problem in West-Central Africa, a specialist on African studies and confusioncracy has made the task easier when he theorizes that "Preponderant evidence portrays Cameroon as properly fitting in both West and Central Africa but the leadership has always only preferred the Central African position" (Fossungu, 2013a: 32). So, you can begin to

---

[19] "[W]e would thus observably be told that there are better *experienced* people for doing the copying from down south. These Canadian-experienced 'professionals' even do the copying without considering us Quebecers who eventually have to go about creating our own French-only versions of programmes like 'Stars Academie', etc. Where then is the national unity that comes with a true sense of belonging with others?" (Fossungu, 2015a: 138)

see then that, while the *Anglospheristic* disease reigns in North America, *Francospheridism* is king in Central Africa. That seems to be the case since "thanks to its Anglophobia, this country [called Cameroon] has traditionally avoided the English-speaking world, and particularly Nigeria; this perhaps also elucidating why it has been active in *La Francophonie* almost from inception but 'bribing its way' into the Commonwealth only in 1995" (Fossungu, 2013a: 34). *Malgre tout cela*, that country still *christikinologically* represents "The Dark Continent" that is bent on "Teaching Americans to Care" (Fossungu, 2015a: 107-111) because "Africa hinges on Cameroon in an assortment of ways that [even America's CIA theorizes that] the country is 'sometimes referred to as the hinge of Africa'" (Fossungu, 2013a: vii).[20] Yes. That clearly is Cameroon uncensored, an indisputable Africa in Miniature. Cameroon thus has all the potentials (and the legitimacy too, perhaps?) to monopolize Africa entirely. But it incomprehensibly restricts itself to just an insignificant part of it: very unlike the *anglosperistic* lovers of North America whose 'red' courts have been incessantly accused of not moving with the times on SSM.

---

[20] In 1986 it was very clearly stated in Cameroon's Objective 29 that "Aware of the fact that a disunited Africa cannot hope to change anything in the world order, we believe that Cameroon should muster all its force so as to contribute to the strengthening of African unity at the continental, regional and sub-regional levels" Paul Biya, *Communal Liberalism* (London: Macmillan, 1986) at 134. See also Ali Mazuri, "Pourquoi les frontières africaines doivent-elles être redessinées?" *Generation* (3-9 juin 1996), 2.

SSM as a Divisive Moral Issue and the Colour of Biology in Homonista: Red Sex and Black?

Many researchers have found that members of the political party associated with the 'red colour' have been very sweeping in their anti-gay declarations, with the critics' conclusion being that "In a nation still battling prejudice against homosexuality, gays and lesbians serve as easy targets for politicians aspiring to appear strong on family values. But political expediency provides poor grounds indeed for continuing to treat a minority unfairly" (Liu and Macedo, 2005: 212). That unfairly-treated minority thesis applies as well to the racial one in America, including one of the Lovings. After their convictions, the Lovings took up residence in the District of Columbia. On November 6, 1963, they filed a motion in the state trial court to vacate the judgment and set aside the sentence on the ground that the statutes which they had violated were repugnant to the Fourteenth Amendment. Their motion not having been decided by October 28, 1964, the Lovings instituted a class action in the United States District Court for the Eastern District of Virginia requesting that a three-judge court be convened to declare the Virginia anti-miscegenation statutes unconstitutional and to enjoin state officials from enforcing their convictions. On January 22, 1965, the state trial judge denied the motion to vacate the sentences, and the Lovings appealed to the Supreme Court of Appeals of Virginia. On February 11, 1965, the three-judge District Court continued the case to allow the Lovings to present their constitutional claims to the highest state court. The Supreme Court of Appeals of Virginia upheld the constitutionality of the anti-miscegenation statutes and, after modifying the sentence, affirmed the convictions. The Lovings appealed this decision to the U.S. Supreme Court which noted probable jurisdiction on December 12, 1966.

Chief Justice Warren stated that the two statutes under which the appellants were convicted and sentenced are part of a comprehensive statutory scheme aimed at prohibiting and punishing interracial marriages. The Lovings were convicted of violating § 258 of the Virginia Code,[21] Section 259 of which defines the penalty for miscegenation and provides: "*Punishment for marriage.* -- If any white person intermarry with a colored person, or any colored person intermarry with a white person, he shall be guilty of a felony and shall be punished by confinement in the penitentiary for not less than one nor more than five years."[22] Other central provisions in the Virginia statutory scheme are § 20-57, which automatically voids all marriages between "a white person and a colored person" without any judicial proceeding, and §§ 20-54 and 1-14 which, respectively, define "white persons" and "colored persons and Indians" for purposes of the statutory prohibitions. The Lovings never disputed in the course of this litigation that Mrs. Loving was a "colored person" or that Mr. Loving was a "white person" within the meanings given those terms by the Virginia statutes.[23] Yes. Fossungu (2015a:

---

[21] *Leaving State to evade law.* -- If any white person and colored person shall go out of this State, for the purpose of being married, and with the intention of returning, and be married out of it, and afterwards return to and reside in it, cohabiting as man and wife, they shall be punished as provided in § 20-59, and the marriage shall be governed by the same law as if it had been solemnized in this State. The fact of their cohabitation here as man and wife shall be evidence of their marriage. 388 U.S. 1 at 5 (1967).

[22] *Ibid.*

[23] *Id.* 5-6.

97-99) educate them on America and its dubious colourful and colourless colours!

Looking at "the connection between biological attributions about blacks and homosexuals and marriage rights for these groups [which] is very apparent and recently appears to have increased in strength" (Haider-Markel and Joslyn, 2005: 237), can one not safely theorize that this momentous inter-racial marriage case paved the way for same-sex marriage since the *Loving* ruling opened the floodgating out of the closets and into the courts? In the 15 or so years before the case, 14 States had repealed laws outlawing interracial marriages: Arizona, California, Colorado, Idaho, Indiana, Maryland, Montana, Nebraska, Nevada, North Dakota, Oregon, South Dakota, Utah, and Wyoming. The first state court to recognize that miscegenation statutes violated the Equal Protection Clause was the Supreme Court of California in *Perez v. Sharp* [32 Cal.2d 711, 198 P.2d 17 (1948)].

Loving v. Virginia (in the country's highest court) raised the question whether the State of Virginia (as any other state[24])

---

[24] After the initiation of this litigation, Maryland repealed its prohibitions against interracial marriage, Md.Laws 1967, c. 6, leaving Virginia and 15 other States with statutes outlawing interracial marriage: Alabama, Ala.Const., Art. 4, § 102, Ala.Code, Tit. 14, § 360 (1958); Arkansas, Ark.Stat.Ann. § 55-104 (1947); Delaware, Del.Code Ann., Tit. 13, § 101 (1953); Florida, Fla.Const., Art. 16, § 24, Fla.Stat. § 741.11 (1965); Georgia, Ga.Code Ann. § 53-106 (1961); Kentucky, Ky.Rev.Stat.Ann. § 402.020 (Supp. 1966); Louisiana, La.Rev.Stat. § 14:79 (1950); Mississippi, Miss.Const., Art. 14, § 263, Miss.Code Ann. § 459 (1956); Missouri, Mo.Rev.Stat. § 451.020 (Supp. 1966); North Carolina, N.C.Const., Art. XIV, § 8, N.C.Gen.Stat. § 14-181 (1953); Oklahoma, Okla.Stat., Tit. 43, § 12 (Supp. 1965); South Carolina, S.C.Const., Art. 3, § 33, S.C.Code Ann. § 20-7 (1962); Tennessee, Tenn.Const., Art. 11, § 14, Tenn.Code Ann. § 36-402 (1955); Texas, Tex.Pen.Code, Art. 492 (1952); West Virginia, W.Va.Code Ann. § 4697 (1961).

could prohibit couples not of the same race from marrying, with the U.S. Supreme Court concluding that marriage was a fundamental right. Chief Justice Warren in his majority opinion stated that "The freedom to marry has long been recognized as one of the vital personal rights essential to the orderly pursuit of happiness by free men" [388 U.S. 1 at 12 (1967)]. Commenting on this statement, some critics have theorized that "Given the similarity between the old miscegenation laws and the bans on same-sex marriage today, it might be just a matter of time before the federal courts begin to recognize same-sex marriage as a fundamental right" (Crehan, 2013: 15). So, does the *Loving* decision represent a precedent relevant to the issue of SSM? This appears to be the case giving that the argument in *Hollingsworth v. Perry* in 2013 – one of the first two same-sex marriage cases to reach the U.S. Supreme Court, *Windsor v. U.S.* (2013) being the other – is based on the *Loving* precedent. In *Hollingsworth* the plaintiff argued in favour of same-sex marriage rights, stating that "The right to marry has always been based on, and defined by, the constitutional liberty to select the partner of one's choice – not on the partner chosen" (Crehan, 2013: 15-16). But not so fast, some other American states seem to be loudly saying: since four years after Virginia's *Loving*, its reasoning was unsuccessfully invoked in Minnesota in *Baker v. Nelson*, most probably due to the morality and divisiveness of SSM.

Same-Sex Marriage: A Divisive Moral Issue with Changing Public Opinion

Of course, it is not idle talking to indicate that Daniel Pinello "found that judges in southern states and those appointed by Republican presidents are not particularly accommodating of gay rights claims" (Crehan, 2013: 33); a well-known "hostility to same-sex families [that] comes from the very top of the executive branch, with a president [like George W. Bush] who denounces judicial efforts to fairly engage the issue of same-sex marriage as 'activism' dangerous to families and children" (Gerstmann, 2005: 219). But the judges have turned out to be different from the politicians no doubt. What has been less commented upon though is that even some appellate courts from "red states" have engaged the question of same-sex marriage much more seriously than other government officials and they have struggled to give a cogent explanation for excluding same-sex couples from marriage (Gerstmann, 2005: 217). The list of all justices of the country's apex court is a very lengthy one but Table 1 here shows all the Supreme Court Chief Judges to date and the Presidents that appointed them, etc.

Table 1: Chief Justices of the Supreme Court of the United States

Name of Chief Justices	State Appointed From	Appointed by President	Judicial Oath Taken	Date Service Terminated
Jay, John	New York	Washington	October 19, 1789	June 29, 1795
Rutledge, John	South Carolina	Washington	August 12, 1795	December 15, 1795
Ellsworth, Oliver	Connecticut	Washington	March 8, 1796	December 15, 1800
Marshall, John	Virginia	Adams, John	February 4, 1801	July 6, 1835
Taney, Roger Brooke	Maryland	Jackson	March 28, 1836	October 12, 1864
Chase,	Ohio	Lincoln	December	May 7, 1873

Salmon Portland			15, 1864	
Waite, Morrison Remick	Ohio	Grant	March 4, 1874	March 23, 1888
Fuller, Melville Weston	Illinois	Cleveland	October 8, 1888	July 4, 1910
White, Edward Douglass	Louisiana	Taft	December 19, 1910	May 19, 1921
Taft, William Howard	Connecticut	Harding	July 11, 1921	February 3, 1930
Hughes, Charles Evans	New York	Hoover	February 24, 1930	June 30, 1941
Stone, Harlan Fiske	New York	Roosevelt, F.	July 3, 1941	April 22, 1946
Vinson, Fred Moore	Kentucky	Truman	June 24, 1946	September 8, 1953
Warren, Earl	California	Eisenhower	October 5, 1953	June 23, 1969
Burger, Warren Earl	Virginia	Nixon	June 23, 1969	September 26, 1986
Rehnquist, William H.	Virginia	Reagan	September 26, 1986	September 3, 2005
Roberts, John G., Jr.	Maryland	Bush, G. W.	September 29, 2005	

Source: http://www.supremecourt.gov/about/members_text.aspx

Putnam and Campbell praise American religious harmony but would agree with other critics that abortion and homosexuality have come to be especially salient in contemporary politics, which in turn has led to a religious divide at the ballot box (Putnam and Campbell, 2012: 22; Patrikios, 2008; Hillygus and Shields, 2005; Lewis, 2005). According to Margaret Gram Crehan, the same-sex marriage issue has been raised in some way in every state in the United States. For instance, as of October 2013, she advances the following theses: That Massachusetts, Connecticut, California, Iowa, Vermont, New Hampshire, New York, Maine, Maryland, Washington, and the District of Columbia had issued marriage licenses to same-sex couples. Rhode Island, Delaware, Hawaii, Illinois, and Minnesota passed same-sex marriage laws in 2013 but they were yet to take effect. New Jersey and Colorado allowed civil unions; California, Oregon, Nevada, and Washington allowed domestic partnerships; Hawaii, Maine, District of Columbia, and Wisconsin allowed a more limited version of domestic partnership. All other states not mentioned above have either a state law or constitutional provision banning same-sex marriage (Crehan, 2013: 25). I have made this information on the states current as of March 2015 (moment of writing), as you will shortly see in the course of my discussing the SSM as a divisive moral issue across the world and the changing public opinion on it.

The division over the SSM issue in America is even more puzzling particularly in the context of other Western democracies that have legalized homosexuality. For example, we significantly learn from Thoreson (2013: 646) that "On 25 October 2012, the British House of Lords held what was hailed as an historic debate regarding the persecution of gay and lesbian persons worldwide. As they condemned criminalization, discrimination, and forced migration, speakers stressed the importance of changing laws and legislation globally. Sounding a note of caution, however, Lord Collins warned that 'even in countries where homosexuality is legal, lesbian and gay people are often subjected to human rights abuses'." Some of the 'countries where homosexuality is legal' include the Netherlands which in 2001 became the first country to allow same-sex couples to marry. Belgium followed suit in 2003 (Crehan, 2013: 28). The Scandinavian countries of Denmark, Norway, and Sweden legalized gay registered partnerships in 1989, 1993, and 1994, respectively; the Netherlands legalized full gay marriage in 2001 (Liu and Macedo, 2005: 212). Between 2002 and 2004, courts in several Canadian provinces held that the opposite-sex definition of marriage was contrary to the 1982 *Canadian Charter of Rights and Freedoms*, leading to the Canadian Supreme Court's 2004 ruling in *Re Same-Sex Marriage* [3 S.C.R. 698, 2004 SCC 79] in favour of same-sex marriage rights (Crehan, 2013: 28), despite heavy criticisms "that it leads the judiciary to usurp functions that are best left to the legislatures and their agencies" (Bogart, 1994: xii). Apparently having been led by the courts, in 2005 the federal government passed legislation providing for same-sex marriage across Canada (Crehan, 2013: 28; Smith, 2005). Same-sex marriage was legalized in Spain in 2005 and in South Africa in 2006. Norway, Sweden, Portugal, Iceland and Argentina also legalized same-sex marriage between 2008 and 2010. In June 2012, Denmark legalized SSM, with France legalizing it in May 2013 (Crehan, 2013: 29). The trend around the globe thus appears to be in favour of recognition of the rights of same-sex couples to marry.

On the other hand, in "the United States, the society that has looked to the courts the most to resolve complex social and political issues, but with little success" (Bogart, 1994: xi) same-sex marriage has provoked very different responses within members of society. This division is mirrored in the vastly different laws and policies in place in the 50 different states of the union, and on the federal level (Crehan, 2013: 29). It could be, as some critics say, that "[i]n designing the institutional matrix for making decisions on rights issues it is a mistake to look for an error-proof solution" (Russell, 1992: 481). This critic could be correct since a U.S. government publication titled "Same-Sex Marriage Laws" which was last reviewed on March 26, 2015 informs us that marriage laws vary from state to state. The states and areas in the U.S. that perform marriages between same-sex couples are: Alaska, Arizona, California, Colorado, Connecticut, Delaware, District of Columbia, Hawaii, Idaho, Illinois, Indiana, Iowa, Kansas, Maine, Maryland, Massachusetts, Minnesota, Missouri, Montana, Nevada, New Hampshire, New Jersey, New Mexico, New York, North Carolina, Oklahoma, Oregon, Pennsylvania, Rhode Island, South Carolina, Utah, Vermont, Virginia, Washington, West Virginia, Wisconsin, and Wyoming.[25] That is, 36 states (plus D.C.) out of 50 states. This clearly is indicative of the changing perception on SSM since the federal government passed the DOMA in 1996.

This unsettling situation in the USA leads inevitably to a scenario where an American is married in some parts of the country but not in others; thus making no sense of the fact that "we are the 'United' States of America" (Crehan, 2013: 8). The whole apparent confusion or illogicality in this

---

25

http://answers.usa.gov/system/templates/selfservice/USAGov/#!portal /1012/article/4109/Same-Sex-Marriage-Laws (accessed on March 26, 2015).

upsetting matter has led some critics to conclude that it is clearly the case of same-sex, different politics in different states of the same country! And all this despite the fact that public opinion on SSM is changing. This is the way one researcher put it in October 2013:

> Public opinion has changed concerning support for same-sex marriage in the United States. In 2010, 49 percent of Americans supported same-sex marriage, while in 2012 that number rose to 60 percent. Perhaps based in part on the changing views of Americans, in 2012, President Obama made front-page news with his statement in support of same-sex marriage. His endorsement came just before a controversial vote in North Carolina that would add a constitutional amendment defining marriage as existing only between a man and a woman. This contrasts with his originally stated stance against same-sex marriage but in support of civil unions for same-sex couples during the 2008 campaign (Crehan, 2013: 28).

It looks like the winds of change experienced in Europe and South Africa have been sweeping through American public opinion in an unstoppable fashion. As Susan Page of *USA Today* indicates,

> By an unprecedented 55%-40%, Americans say marriages between same-sex couples should be recognized by law as valid, with the same rights of traditional marriage. That's the highest level of support since Gallup began asking the question in 1996. Then, fewer than half that number, 27%, backed the idea.

Last year [2012] was the first time a majority of Americans had backed gay marriage.

The only major demographic groups in which a majority oppose same-sex marriage are Republicans (68%) and seniors 65 and older (51%). Even in the South, which continues to be the only region that doesn't show majority support for gay marriage, opposition has slipped below 50%.

By a narrower margin, 48%-43%, those surveyed favor the Supreme Court's decision [in *Windsor v. U.S.*] declaring unconstitutional part of the 1996 Defense of Marriage Act, which barred the federal government from providing benefits to same-sex spouses. Views on the issue are intense. Those who feel strongly about the issue split 29%-29% in favor and against the ruling (Page, 2013).

Many polls, a few of which are shown in Table 2, will corroborate what these commentators are saying.

Table 2: Sample Polls on Same-Sex Marriage, Gay Rights[26]

ABC News/Washington Post Poll. May 29-June 1, 2014. N=1,002 adults nationwide.
Margin of error ± 3.5.
"Overall, do you support or oppose allowing gays and lesbians to marry legally?"

	Support %	Oppose %	Unsure %
5/29 - 6/1/14	56	38	6
Democrats	67	28	5
Republicans	37	57	6
Independents	58	37	5
2/27 - 3/2/14	59	34	7
6/5-9/13	57	40	3
5/1-5/13	55	40	5

26 Source: http://www.pollingreport.com/civil.htm.

Gallup Poll. May 8-11, 2014. N=1,028 adults nationwide. Margin of error ± 4.

"Do you think marriages between same-sex couples should or should not be recognized by the law as valid, with the same rights as traditional marriages?"

	Should %	Should not %	Unsure %
5/8-11/14	55	42	3
7/10-14/13	54	43	3
5/2-7/13	53	45	3
11/26-29/12	53	46	2
5/3-6/12	50	48	2
12/15-18/11	48	48	4
5/5-8/11	53	45	3
5/3-6/10	44	53	3
5/7-10/09	40	57	3
5/8-11/08	40	56	4
5/10-13/07	46	53	1
5/8-11/06	42	56	2

ABC News/Washington Post Poll. Oct. 9-12, 2014. N=1,006 adults nationwide. Margin of error ± 3.5.

"Do you support or oppose the Supreme Court action this week that allows gay marriages to go forward in several more states?"

	Support %	Oppose %	Unsure %
ALL	56	38	6
Democrats	72	23	5
Republicans	25	64	11
Independents	63	32	5

With these obvious 'Marriage and Shifting Priorities' (Egan and Sherrill, 2005), some critics just cannot understand why, despite the enormous public support for anti-discrimination measures in employment for lesbian and gay citizens, as well as scholarly analysis in good turn, there is instead a "Diffusion of Support for Same-Sex Marriage in the US Senate" (Theriault and Thomas III, 2014), which leads to the fact that, as Fossungu (2015a: 132) cites a critic for saying, 'even simple anti-discrimination measures are not in force in most U.S. states. While Canada is legalizing same-sex marriage, the U.S. has debated and passed state and federal constitutional amendments to ban same-sex marriages.' The "constitutional amendments" being talking about include the 1996 DOMA, the passage of which "highlighted the federalism aspects of the issue of SSM in the United States" (Crehan, 2013: 31). How do the courts view such comportment of the other branches?

Minnesota Marries Procreation and Constitutionality while Hawaii Provokes Congress to Violate the Constitution?

Minnesota's *Baker v. Nelson:* "Be careful what you ask for," goes the old adage, according to Patrick J. Egan and Kenneth Sherrill, because "You just might get it." This advice, they say, is well-taken by interest groups that successfully press for policy goals at odds with the preferences of the broader population. Victory may be won, but at the expense of awakening widespread opposition and aggravating friend and foe alike (Egan and Sherrill, 2005: 229). Most critics agree that this contentious same-sex marriage issue (that Utah and South Dakota were, respectively, the first and second states to ban SSM - Crehan, 2013: 17) could begin with *Baker*, when Jack Baker and Mike McConnell attempted to marry in Minnesota under the theory that since there was no specific prohibition against same-sex marriage, the legislature must have intended to allow it (Crehan, 2013: 13-14).

One can see the validity of the 'Beware what you ask for' thesis in the way politicians like Senator John Kerry (and even ordinary people from the states concerned) are often treated immediately after the homosexuals' breakthrough in cases like *Goodridge v. Massachusetts Department of Health* (2003) and *Lawrence v. Texas* (2003). With the exception of Massachusetts (where polling in the state around the time of the court decision found near-majorities in support of same-sex marriage), in the states where these rulings have been handed down, gay activists have found themselves advocating for gay marriage with a distinct disadvantage in public opinion. In other states—41 of which have recoiled in horror at these rulings to take some sort of action banning same-sex marriage since the mid-1990s— activists have fought against these proposals without being able to explicitly advocate for gay marriage (Egan and Sherrill, 2005: 229).

Goodridge v. Massachusetts Department of Health (2003) took place 30 years after Baker and McConnell were denied a marriage license based on the fact that they were the same sex. They had first brought suit in a lower Minnesota court claiming that the Minnesota Statute did not specifically require that the applicants be of different sexes. They also argued that if the Court found that the statute did have this intent, then it violated the First Amendment's freedom of speech and association, the Eighth Amendment's prohibition against cruel and unusual punishment, the Ninth

Amendment's un-enumerated right to privacy and the Fourteenth Amendment because there was a fundamental right to marry under the Due Process Clause and sex discrimination is contrary to the Equal Protection Clause.

The Minnesota Supreme Court first examined the statute itself and the common usage of the term "marriage" and found that other references were gender-specific and thus the statute did prohibit marriage between persons of the same-sex. But the Court distinguished certain marriage cases like *Loving v. Virginia*, finding that there is a clear distinction between a marital restriction based on race, and those based on the fundamental difference in sex. The court's conclusion was "that the statute did not violate the Due Process clause because procreation and child rearing were central to the constitutional protection of marriage" (Crehan, 2013: 14). Similarly, it has been discovered that "very few are the African men who get married without the central issue being to have children" (Fossungu, 2013c: 157). It seems as if the *Baker* court was here considering only one or two of the purposes of marriage as discussed in Fossungu (2015a: 149-150).[27] This procreation question is further pursued (in chapter 5) in the *Goodrige* case that was inspired by Hawaii's *Baehr*.

Goodridge would later embrace the social purpose of marriage to the total abandonment of the others, with the

---

[27] As a Church and family expert also noted in 2010, "Westermarck then contends that the development of marriage among humans was less about the relationship between the husband and the wife and more a matter of raising offspring. Thus there are other theories about the origin of marriage that suggest that marriage was a way of ensuring that procreative activities would be successful which would in return increase the likelihood of survival for all men, women and children" (cited in Fossungu, 2015a: 29).

courts of the southern states of Arizona and of Indiana (even after *Goodridge* and *Lawrence*) still focusing on "the inability of same-sex couples to bear children via sexual intercourse" (Gerstmann, 2005: 218). This *Morrison v. Sadler* dictum was the same position taken in the Kentucky Supreme Court case of *James v. Hallahan* that also came after *Baker*. These 'Red Courts' are seemingly trying to uphold the myth drawn from the 'Adam-Eve-Intention' of God. Indeed, one can accurately compare them to "some parents [who] are still clearly oblivious of the fact that their children are born in an era that is very different from theirs. For instance, some time ago, a man with many wives (mostly, if not completely, chosen by his own parents) had little or no problems governing his *foyer*. Not exactly so today with just two or three wives that he has himself selected" (Fossungu, 2014: 86).

Yes. These red courts are somewhat oblivious of being in a country and era where not only a God-Gap exists but also a whole new deity called CAPITAL or MONEY. America is money-driven, no doubt about that. As Evan Gerstmann has interestingly noted, having these procreation-based cases in mind,

For same-sex couples seeking access to the institution of marriage, the public sense that marriage is naturally and obviously meant only for opposite-sex couples has been a formidable barrier. The first state supreme courts to rule on same-sex marriage, in the early 1970s, simply relied upon dictionary definitions to hold that marriage was obviously a heterosexual institution. Politicians mostly ignored the issue altogether until the courts of Hawaii, Vermont, and Massachusetts forced public debate of the issue (Gertsmann, 2005: 217, note omitted).

The Impact of Hawaii's *Baehr v. Lewin*: The MPA, DOMA Challenges, FMA and the Preaching of Morals on Capitol Hill?

Baker's petition for a writ of certiorari from the U.S. Supreme Court was denied for failure to present a federal question. Clearly, this refusal decision is telling us that marriage issues are the states' province, not for the federal government as is the case in Canada (see chapter 5). To better bring the federalism/unconstitutionality question out, let's take the Marriage Protection Act (MPA) of 2005 that was supported by President George W. Bush and which was meant to strip the federal courts of jurisdiction over challenges to the DOMA and block access to the legal system for gays and lesbians. The relevant text of the MPA states:

§ 1632. Limitation on jurisdiction

No court created by Act of Congress shall have any jurisdiction, and the Supreme Court shall have no appellate jurisdiction, to hear or decide any question pertaining to the interpretation of, or the validity under the Constitution of, section 1738C of this section (cited in Crehan, 2013: 24).

Absent the unconstitutionality theory, it is thus not clear what one is to make of all the court challenges to DOMA, ultimately reaching the United States Supreme Court. According to Margaret Gram Crehan, the same-sex marriage issue began its journey to the federal courts as the constitutionality of the DOMA and of California's Proposition 8 went before the U.S. Supreme Court in March 2013 in the cases of *Windsor* and *Hollingsworth*. Earlier in 2009,

Massachusetts was the first state to file in federal court seeking to have DOMA ruled unconstitutional. In 2010, a District Court in Massachusetts ruled against DOMA, a decision that was upheld by a First Circuit Court of Appeals three-judge panel in May 2012. On the heels of this ruling, Crehan points out, the Bipartisan Legal Advisory Group (BLAG), appointed by the Republican majority in the U.S. House of Representatives, filed an appeal asking the Court to reverse the lower court ruling. Normally a case such as this one would be litigated by the Attorney General of the U.S., however, the Obama Administration stated that it would not defend DOMA (Crehan, 2013: 25-26).

The question is: What has happened to the 2005 MPA that was intended to withdraw federal courts' jurisdiction in the matter? The answer could reside in the fact that even the proponents of the MPA knew that it was unconstitutional to impose federal regulation on marriage that is a state domain. One expert summarizes the Supreme Court's reasoning as follows:

In March 2013, oral arguments were presented in both the DOMA and Prop. 8 case[s]. The role of federalism in the SSM cases is evident from the Justices themselves. During oral argument in the Prop 8 case, Justice Anthony Kennedy, considered the possible swing vote for the issue, expressed his federalism-based concerns in the following way, "The question is whether or not the federal government under our federalism scheme has the authority to regulate marriage." And in the DOMA case, Justice Sonia Sotomayor asked, "What gives the federal government the right to be concerned at all about what the definition of marriage is?" The Federalism argument goes even deeper when we consider the fact that the Obama Administration decided that it would not defend DOMA (Crehan, 2013: 150).

But the never-going-away question relates to whether the courts always follow their own judgments. That is, do they follow *stare decisis* which some experts have described as being the principal norm of the American legal system? It does not appear to be the case since *Lawrence* did not follow but instead overturn its predecessor. Again, a different story is told by the spate of cases since the 1993 case of *Baehr v. Lewin* or "the [Hawaiian] state court decision on same-sex marriage that provoked Congress to enact the Defense of Marriage Act in 1996" (Crehan, 2013: 16).

Some critics have pointed out that the DOMA was passed by an overwhelming majority in Congress (three hundred and forty-two to sixty-seven in the House and eighty-five to fourteen in the Senate) and was signed into law by President Bill Clinton. But why did the FMA fail to pass in Congress unlike the DOMA that easily passed in both Houses? According to some writers, the idea for an FMA did not suddenly dawn upon Senate Republicans in the summer of 2004, when debate on the amendment began in earnest on the floor of the U.S. Senate. Despite the passage of the federal DOMA in 1996, conservatives have long worried about what they believe are the threats to traditional heterosexual marriage posed by the courts. In July 2004, the FMA, sponsored by Republican Senator Wayne Allard of Colorado, reached the Senate floor. As introduced, the amendment read: "Marriage in the United States shall consist only of the union of a man and a woman. Neither this Constitution, nor the constitution of any State, shall be construed to require that marriage or the legal incidents thereof be conferred upon any union other than the union of a man and a woman." After four days of debate, Republican senators failed to persuade enough of their colleagues to support the FMA; the Senate fell 12 votes short of the 60 needed to invoke closure on the motion to proceed to the amendment (Liu and Macedo, 2005: 211).

One prominent reason why the FMA failed has to do with the lack of public outcry against the *Lawrence* decision, which reflected shifts in public opinion toward acceptance or at least tolerance of homosexuality. As the critics explain, in the aftermath of *Lawrence* the Republicans' objective was to establish a new reasoned basis for limiting marriage to heterosexuals: to justify the FMA without condemning private homosexual conduct between consenting adults (Liu and Macedo, 2005: 211). Another cause relates to selective targeting of homosexuals as unfit parents by the proponents of the Act. It was not a smart move as some commentators explain:

> If traditional heterosexual marriage is the ideal setting for raising children as Republican senators claimed, the government is still not justified in depriving same-sex couples of the benefits of marriage. That same-sex relations fall short of the ideal for parenting does not render them shameful, let alone immoral. Why, then, should the government regard homosexual marriages as unworthy of recognition? (Liu and Macedo, 2005: 211)

A lot of critics find it hard to understand Congress' action in regard of DOMA. But this is not the case among the experts on American Religion. Some of these commentators have suggested that it is because of Americans' religiosity, views that must be reflected in Washington, that the voices of homosexuals are not listened to there. That is exactly right. The courts thus remain the places of hope, with Larry Kramer (long-time New York City gay activist, speaking after the November 2004 re-election of George W. Bush) charging (as cited in Smith, 2005: 225) that "Nobody listens to us. There is not a single person in Washington who will get us... anything but shit and more shit. I'm sorry. This is where we are now. Nowhere." The fact is that congressional scholars have for several decades "all but ignored asking questions about the potential influence of religion on Congress and its members" (Black, Koopman and Hawkins, 2011: 272).

There has been a conscious effort, including among Republicans, on Capitol Hill to avoid adopting the sort of "intolerant" and "moralistic" tone often associated with the "Religious Right." Nevertheless, researchers have found some interesting trends through interviewing staff on the Hill. As their report indicates,

One Republican legislative assistant admitted that his senator eliminated references to Judeo-Christian values that appeared in the original draft of his floor statement on the FMA. Another Republican aide spoke of her senator as "a religious man" who took a position against gay marriage first and "put words to it" later—words that never mentioned the influence of his faith. And yet another staffer conceded that, while her Republican senator's religious views were important in determining his stance on same-sex marriage, the senator could not reveal them and risk appearing "homophobic" before his constituents (Liu and Macedo, 213-214, note omitted).[28]

---

[28] For more extensive discussions on 'Religion and Congress', see Black, Koopman and Hawkers, 2011: chapter 8; and Oldmixon, 2011.

In view of an incisive 2014 study on 'The Diffusion of Support for Same-Sex Marriage in the US Senate' (Theriault and Thomas III, 2014), it is thus a grave error not to realize that "[b]ecause so many of the American people are religious, one set of public values quite plausibly reflected in Washington is religious values" (Black, Koopman and Hawkins, 2011: 271). With that knowledge, the reaction to *Baehr* on Capitol Hill, as well as the Clinton White House, is easily grasped, although some critics argue that it is more of a matter of "the courts [being] well out in front in terms of moving past the reflexive notion that marriage simply has to be opposite-sex" (Gerstmann, 2005: 217).

Reversing *Baehr v. Lewin* Equals to Rejecting *Marbury* and Marshall?

In December 1990, three same-sex couples – Nina Baehr (Baehr), Genora Dancel (Dancel), Tammy Rodrigues (Rodrigues), Antoinette Pregil (Pregil), Pat Lagon (Lagon), and Joseph Melilio (Melilio) (collectively "the plaintiffs") – filed marriage applications (notably without the support of a national LGBT legal agency[29]) at the Department of Health in Honolulu. The Department's denial of their applications led to a legal battle that would last six years. In 1993, the Hawaiian Supreme Court ruled that in light of the Hawaii

---

[29] LGBT stands for Lesbians, Gays, Bisexuals and Transgender. Leaving out the 'T' (in LGBT) in his article that discusses trans and intersex persons, Thoreson (2013: 647) explains that "LGB identities arise from sexual orientation toward partners of the same or multiple genders. They are distinct from trans identities, which are rooted in gender identity and expression, or intersex identities, which are rooted in biological sex. Some trans persons are also intersex, some trans and intersex persons are also LGB, and some people fit into one category but not the others."

Constitution's equal protection clause, which explicitly prohibits discrimination on the basis of sex, the lower court's decision against the plaintiffs' claims of discrimination was in error and remanded the case. The Court held that marriage was a fundamental right that triggered the highest standard of review – strict scrutiny – and went on to state that,

> The statute pertaining to marriage in Hawaii is presumed to be unconstitutional unless Lewin, as an agent of the State of Hawaii, can show that (a) the statute's sex-based classification is justified by compelling state interests and (b) is narrowly drawn to avoid unnecessary abridgments of the applicant couple's constitutional rights (Crehan, 2013: 16).

Thus the Supreme Court of Hawaii did find that under the state's equal protection clause, denying marriage licenses to same-sex couples constituted discrimination. But, before any ruling went into effect, Hawaii voters passed an Amendment to the state constitution that allowed the state to reserve marriage for opposite sex couples, an "effort to overturn a decision of the state's highest court by popular initiative [that] will be repeated again by other states" (Crehan, 2013: 17). Without a grasp of the reversal arguments evident in the FMA and the discussion in chapter 1, it would appear that what actually took place in Hawaii after the *Baehr* ruling plainly contradicts Chief Justice Marshall's dictum in *Marbury v. Madison* in 1803:

> So if a law be in opposition to the constitution; if both the law and the constitution apply to a particular case, so that the court must either decide that case

conformably to the law, disregarding the constitution; or conformably to the constitution, disregarding the law; the court must determine which of these conflicting rules governs the case. This is of the very essence of judicial duty.

If, then, the courts are to regard the constitution, and the constitution is superior to any ordinary act of the legislature, the constitution, and not such ordinary act, must govern the case to which they both apply (*How the Court Became Supreme*).

We thus can see that the highway to Hawaii was not to "nowhere" as some might think. Even though *Baker v. Nelson* failed in 1971 to claim the gains of *Loving* to itself, *Baehr* certainly gave the push needed for the Massachusetts bomb-dropping decision in *Goodridge v. Massachusetts Department of Health* (2003), described by some experts as "the case that cleared the way for Massachusetts to become the first state to marry same-sex couples" (Egan and Sherrill, 2005: 229). We will be discussing this milestone case in chapter 5 after chapters 3 and 4 have dissected deception and the political economy of deaths, births and marriages within another kind of NNA African family called the Cameroon Goodwill Association of Montreal (CGAM).

Chapter 3

Deception and the Political Economy of Deaths in a Northern North American West-Central African Family

Dear Goodwillers, Heartfelt Thanks for the massive and proactive participation in the meeting. The quality of the discussions, the reciprocal respect for each other, and our focus on issues not individuals demonstrate that Goodwill has a high sense of quality rather than quantity. It was just wonderful to share with our special visitors as well as our out-of-town members, Jules and Claire [Komguep]. We should continue to be proud members of Goodwill [Fidelis Folefac, CGAM President, thanking CGAMers on October 11, 2009].

The chapter is in three parts. The first is a survey on death, witchcraft and the CGAM. The second deals with the manner of coping with death while the third examines the operation of the Death Social Packages, including how the Death of a Member (CGAMer) is handled within the CGAM family.

On Death, Witchcraft and the CGAM: *Josephizationing* Death Theorists and Spree

The Death Theorists of the Family: On recounting his harrowing experiences with a hungry beast in the forest, the lucky survivor came to the theory that "I think it could just be summarized by saying that if death had to be seen coming, even the lame and *footless* would get up and escape from its no-release grip" (Fossungu, 2015b: 144, original emphasis).

Death has some inexplicable powers in both Life and Death. As Fon DF Fossungu of Nwangong put it in October 2002 during the funeral ceremony of Chief Forbehndia (Emmanuel Nguajong Fossungu), "It is not like the first to come is always the first to go because death has its canny way of operating. All I can tell you right now is just that everyone who came will one day also go. Where exactly they go to, I can hardly say since we can never know what happens on the other side. No one has ever returned from there to explain that to us." I then immediately recalled the deceased's own 'Book of Life and Death' question to his wife (see Fossungu, 2013c: 28) and began wondering if my family is 'brimatized' with excellent theorists on death.

The Fon's words suddenly assumed a pronounced signification to me when his other brother, Chief Foletia, later advised that "You can never know when exactly to expect death's knock on the door. Therefore, if there is anything you want to do, just go ahead and do it and stop procrastinating and saying 'I will, I will, I will'. Because, while you are doing that, death is calculating your days and laughingly saying on its part: 'He doesn't know my calendar and can never be aware that I am coming for him this very night'. So, my brethren, as we are here gathered to bid Chief Forbehndia farewell, my counsel to you is that if there is a piece of kola nut in your pocket, do share it with the one next to you and don't say you will do so only tomorrow...."

Fon DF Fossungu could be right about the other side of death. But it is comforting, at least, that we know what occurs on this side, in the sense that when the death thief strikes, it can either strengthen the family left behind or destroy it. The destructive option is aggravated by the fact that in Africa, for example, death is hardly perceived as a normal ecosystemic or 'come-and-go' occurrence that could be independent of *africanscience*. Akoh Asa'na, in his posting to the SobaAmerica Forum on Friday, 6 March 2015 at 11:05:33 AM, proffered the following food for thought:

Why must everything be explained only in terms of witchcraft? A drunken driver has an accident that kills many of his passengers – it's witchcraft! An *okada* carrying 4 passengers has an accident-- it's witchcraft! A student is stabbed and killed in Sasse -- it's witchcraft! A man abandons his family for a new girlfriend-- it's witchcraft! A young girl who doesn't know how to swim, drowns -- it must be witchcraft. If you make too much money --it's witchcraft. If you're too broke and your family members are dead -- it's witchcraft.

Nothing whatsoever has ever been given the amount of powers we attribute to witchcraft! Not even God!

If there's witchcraft use it to fight Boko Haram, Ebola, HIV (which we're now told originated from Cameroon). Use your witchcraft to punish those police officers who humiliate and harass travelers daily. Where is this witchcraft when we needed it the most? When white people were taking our brothers and sisters as slaves or expropriating land to create cash crop plantations?

Please excuse my ranting. But the time has come for us as a people to bury this anachronistic myth called witchcraft.

Most things can be explained rationally. Witchcraft has become the de facto explanation for everything we don't understand. But we have experts today in various fields who may shed the light on these issues.[30]

***Josephization* on Mother's Death: A Family Deception Classic?** *Africanscience* is too often used to explain death in Africa but death itself also has been employed as explanation of other happenings, real or imagined. This appears to be the case in Momany's family when his mother (who brought him up) died in 1998 while he was in NNA. As you can see, death in the family can provoke the worst in some family members as exemplified by Joseph's letter here that most people would also brand as a classic in family deception. Joseph's undated letter to his father is not only extremely rude but very confusing too, especially to those who know the indicted parties well. A copy of Joe's letter whose only address-line is "Joseph Njumo USA" was sent to Momany (by Papa Emmanuel in his own letter of November 6, 1998) and reads:

> Emmanuel, I hope you are still alive on the arrival of this letter. This note is just to let you know what I thought cause my mother's death and how I feel about it.

---

[30] See "Re: SobaAmerica Cameroon Under Occultic Manipulation." On Friday, March 6, 2015 at 2:53 PM, Kevin Y Njabo wrote in response:

Thank you Akoh Asa'na for highlighting this very important issue. It's easier to look for an escape route or fast closure to a problem and hide everything behind the so-called witch craft. I'm sorry to say even our learned colleagues justify inept behavior behind witch craft!!! Our society wallows in ignorance - not just a blank space on our mental map, but from your examples below, we see contours and coherence in many respects. Mr. Akoson, 'The Order of Valour' is an order of knighthood in Cameroon and the ribbon of the order is red, which is being displayed by officials on their suit breast. It has nothing to do with secret society to which they belong. I just hope we'll carefully read the mail from Asa'na again and ask why.

She was a great woman who gave you all the respect she could and had so many children with you only to be abandoned by you when you met a public prostitute called Catherine. She died because of mental torture from you and your stupid Fosungu people. She died from heart attack because your so-called "Angel" (Catherine) poisoned your mind with lies. She (Catherine) wants nothing but your wealth. Tell her I say she has done a good job, but the worst is still to come. I am a blood man. I wouldn't mind risking my life in prison for what I stand for and believe in. [T]ell her (Catherine) to hope I die soon, for she is going to be sorry.

Emmanuel, you used to be a Father before you met this bitch called Catherine. You extended your problems at home to innocent Joe; I am talking about me. You lost your senses when you met this bitch named Catherine. You made yourself a public idiot and a lunatic. You disgraced all your children and the entire Fosungu and Njumo Family including the entire Nwa-Mundani; you are a disgrace to the entire Bangwa tribe. You set a very bad example to your children and you still think you are a Father. Emmanuel, I am talking to you!

Teresa and Catherine poison your mind to the extent that you abandoned my mother and caused her death. She didn't even want to [talk to] anybody because [she] said she wanted to keep on drinking and "die and go". You used to blame all my problems with you on my mother. I know [that] your Catherine, Teresa and the entire Fosungu family (some few excluded) are happy she is dead. I know you all shared [sic] crocodile tears. Why did you burry her in the Fosungu village? Did you like her? Did your Fosungu people like her? Shame on you!

You used to blame everything on her. You took me all the way to the village just to tell me you have abandoned my mother. Perhaps you thought I loved you more than my mother because you sent me to America. I grew up with my mother in the kitchen. You killed my mother. Catherine killed my mother. I have paid you for sending me to America by leaving my land for my junior sisters. One of them will come here when the land is sold. *As from next year I will start working on the process of bringing Gladys here in [sic] the U.S.A. you are not my father anymore.* I promise[d] Gladys I will start trying to make sure she comes as of January next year.

You used to blame everything on my mother, who are you going to blame it on? You[r] late mother? I know your father was a very-very good man, a man of great personality. I regret he wasn't there when you started acting like a fool. I know his soul has rested in perfect peace. Before I forget, I know you have written your "WILL" and my name is not on it. Do me a favour, if my name is there, change your "WILL". Take my name off!

I will continue from where I ended. Who are you going to blame my problem with you on now that my mother is dead? You told Marie-Claire's husband you like me because I speak out my mind. You are a hypocrite, you don't like me and you didn't like my mother. You ought to be ashame[d] of yourself. Now I think you have to blame everything on your late mother. She was nothing but a bitch and that makes you a son of a bitch. I know you like to fuck and I know you fuck Teresa too. Fuck her good and fuck her in her anus like you fuck Catherine. Fuck her and have children with her since Catherine cannot have children anymore and my mother is dead. Before you die put in your "WILL" that when you die, Catherine should be buried with you alive so that you will be fucking her in your grave. Our mother live[d] for so long and had grandchildren, for how long did your mother live? I think your mother died when you were born. You don't even know her name. Shame on you! You are going to hell. Get good lawyers for on the judgement day you will be in trouble. But there is one thing I really hope for – your death. I hope you die very soon so everything becomes equal. You are a son of a bitch! You are a mad man Emmanuel! I don't care if I die now, son of a bitch. It is a good thing your mother died at a very early age for you could have been fucking her too. Your mother was a bitch because she was fucking every man.

Joseph – Njumo USA. [Emphasis and capitals are original]

CGAM and Its Death Spree: Wow! Death can really steal a lot out of the living, making the sane management of death a sine qua non? It looks very much like the midnightly nailing of the death nail into the harmonious-progressive fabric of the CGAM also opened up the death-spree. From the Financial Secretariat on August 14, 2009 came loudly ringing this call to order to 'Dear Members':

This year like last year is very trying to us regarding financial contributions. Despite the financial relief package the Executive came up with, permit me to remark that **the amount members still owe for death assistance contributions is alarmingly high (over $1,200 – see list below).** We understand that times are hard but we believe God will provide to enable us honour our commitment to support members morally and financially when there is a need. See list below for what you owe and make an effort to make your contribution.

On a different note, **members are reminded of the wake-keep[ing] in honour of KIZITO's mom (see SG's mail below for details). Contributions are required to come in today during the wake keep[ing]. ($30/member rounded for simplicity** and to avoid the meeting always being at a loss position since 100% contribution seems not to be a reality). [List omitted here] The Financial Secretary [capitals, bold & underlining are original]

The above communication is simply meant to give you an idea of what is known in the CGAM as "the social packages" (*sociopackism*) which would relate to death, birth and marriage assistance when a member is affected by any one of them. (They are intertwined but birth and marriages are examined in the next chapter.) It is not just about the financial contribution alone that we are talking about here because the Financial Secretary was in this particular instance, following up with Secretary-General Rita Ewane's further enlightening communication of August 13, 2009.[31]

---

[31] The communiqué read:
    HELLO ALL,
WE ARE SORRY FOR THE SHORT NOTICE. FOLLOWING THE DEATH OF THE MUM OF ONE OF US, A WAKE KEEPING IS SCHEDULED FOR TOMORROW FRIDAY AUGUST 14 AT THE FOLLOWING ADDRESS: 9758 St Patrick Appt 301 LaSalle QC H8R1S2 Tel: 514-[XXX-YYYY] Time: 8 pm
    LADIES AND GENTLEMEN, WE COUNT ON EACH OTHER FOR SUPPORT DURING SAD AND JOYFUL EVENTS. WE ARE THEREFORE ADVISED TO COME IN OUR NUMBERS TO

Battling with Death: Prayerful *Thankyouology* and Useful Lessons from Excellent Comforters

Deaths have at times seemed to almost overwhelm CGAMers. At the same time these sad events have not failed to engender and solidify the communal solidarity that Africans are well noted for. A visionary CGAM president on June 9, 2006 aptly described all these things in his '*When It Rains, It Pours*' message, making known that:

> The Goodwill family has recently been overcome by bereavements, and many members of the Goodwill family are in mourning. At times like this, the Goodwill family becomes one, united in the grief of its members. The many messages that have flooded this site bear testimony to this spirit of goodwill. To all those in mourning, I would like to reiterate that your loss is our loss; the entire Goodwill family is with you at this difficult time. We all join in wishing that the Lord may comfort you at this time of loss and that soul of the dearly departed may rest in perfect peace.

I think the most important reasons for such astounding coping capacity have to do with a couple of things, two of which are prayer and *thankyouology*. A typical CGAM Meeting

---

SUPPORT KISSITO AT THIS VERY DIFFICULT MOMENT OF HIS LIFE.

NOTE: WOMEN, BRING COOKED FOOD AND MEN, COME ALONG WITH DRINKS.

THE FINANCIAL DESK WILL LET US KNOW HOW MUCH EACH MEMBER IS TO CONTRIBUTE TO MAKE UP $1500 (FINANCIAL SUPPORT). **PLEASE [COME] ALONG WITH YOUR CONTRIBUTIONS.**

RITA. PEACE [paragraphing altered; capitals and bold are original].

Agenda always embodies five elements (with a sixth that, for quite some time, almost became standard): (1) Opening prayer, (2) Adoption of agenda, (3) Adoption of minutes of previous meeting, (4) Announcements, (5) Any other matter, (and (6) Topic of discussion). Prayer is a notable hallmark of CGAM activities. We all know the well-known idiom that *heaven helps those who help themselves*. Some people do not quite grasp the proper meaning of the slogan. But Bendrix Tabu broke it down quite well when he wrote on 25 March 2015 at 4.04 PM to the SobaAmerica Forum (in response to Rev. Epizitome's message), explaining that:

> ... Different opinions need to be heard, including yours which was well stated, and which took a trajectory that is unfortunately absent at some crucial moments. I am talking about your invocation of love, faith, prayer, and God. .... We cannot sit and do nothing, and afterwards call on God to come to our rescue, come the time for us to face the consequences of any actions of ours, or lack thereof. Rev., you know that Jesus taught the people to give to Cesar what belongs to Cesar, so should we [not] obey the Canadian and USA laws[?] A willful disregard of the law today, with the knowledge of its consequence, and then imploring God's intervention in the phase of retribution, could be seen as a mockery to His abundant grace. Brother, the Lord also allows punishment when he choose[s] .....

Not waiting until things actually go wrong before turning around to blame heaven for not helping, is a virtue worth cultivating. And you also clearly see it at work in Momany's self-help initiatives communicated to his father on November

16, 1995. "Dear father", he lengthily and *thankyouologistically* wrote:

> I hope you are well. What about your legs? And, everyone there with you, too?
>
> Pa, I appreciate the financial problems my coming over here to Canada has dragged you into. I am aware that if I have to continue relying on you till the end of this course then I shall be driving you into your grave earlier than would normally have been the case. It is really rough with me here and would likely continue to be so for quite some years to come. But I trust what I am about to propose would be quite reasonable and acceptable to you.
>
> I have just received (yesterday) two thousand five hundred dollars ($2500) from your bank. Thank you very much for it. I would, however, plead with you to instruct them to further send, as soon as they possibly can, three thousand five hundred dollars ($3500) to help me pay my fees for this semester (as the attached slip can show) which ends December 1995. Pa, if you could just help me clear this semester's fees, then I promise to do the rest myself (i.e., I shall struggle as much as I can with the rest myself). Next semester I shall have to pay the expenses myself without having to call on you as I am now doing.
>
> Of course, I know the difficulty that I would be facing henceforth but I think that to have all the money that was blocked sent here so that I speedily terminate the course, get a job (if that could be as easy as it may seem anyway) and then send back the money would create more problems to you than the difficulties I shall surely face by having just six thousand dollars (about half of it)

sent to me – with the rest standing by for meeting some of your numerous meeting responsibilities. I hope you can see the sense in this proposal. To have that money tied up for one year will be useless as the bank has already cut its due sums for effecting the authorized transfers that they are obliged to effect on demand. To have all that money sent to me here will certainly, I understand, create you a lot of problems, even if I have to refund it a year or so later. I am in serious financial difficulties here as no other persons but you are responsible for my being here. But being already here, I have to fight for myself and give you breathing time and space.

I am, therefore, dispatching a letter also to the bank requesting three thousand five hundred ($3500) dollars and instructing them at the same time to thereafter release the reminder of the blocked sum. Please do go down there and make sure that the remainder is not less than two million two hundred and fifty thousand (2,250,000) francs CFA. Let me explain why I say so. The Embassy converted the totality to be twelve thousand five hundred dollars ($12,500). If six thousand is taken away the remainder must be six thousand five hundred, which is more than half. Remember the bank had already cut charges for transferring the four million five hundred so they cannot now say they have cut charges from the amount. Therefore, on release of the remainder, you must have an amount superior to two million two hundred and fifty (2,250,000) francs CFA.

I will start my examinations for the semester on 8th December 1995 and the results may not be released to me until I have settled my fees. As you can see, 230 dollars 03 cents have already entered as interest (or penalty) and the later the higher the interest (or penalty) rises.

I have to end here with a request that you extend my warm greetings to Madam Catherine, Mami Cecilia, Valentine, Mr. Ndango and family, all the children at home in Yoke and Limbe (when you next see them), Mr. Bilong and family, Mr. Philip and family, etc.

God will surely bless us all. Your son, Peter.[32]

Africans as Classical *Thankyouologists*

Success in stress management in the CGAM, no doubt, is also attributed to the dynamism of members, especially when it comes to involving themselves in members' diverse activities. To fully document this statement of fact would

---

[32] The abovementioned letter to the bank, written on the same day (November 16, 1995), was addressed to 'The Manager of the SGBC Limbe Branch' and read as follows:

Sir, I wish to let you know that I have received through my account (04461-003-505-625-4) the sum of two thousand five hundred (Canadian) dollars (2500). I noticed this yesterday just when I was about dropping a letter to you into the mail. Thank you very much for that dispatch.

By this present letter, I also wish to:

1. Request that a further three thousand five hundred dollars be sent to enable me clear my fees as the attached photocopy of slip indicates. On numerous occasions I have tried reaching you by phone to no avail, always getting the busy line signal every time.

2. Authorize SGBC Limbe Branch, after operation No. 1 above, to release, with immediate effect, the remainder of the sum of money (that was blocked to my benefit) to the exclusive benefit of my father, Mr. Fosungu Emmanuel Nguajong, holder of SGBC Limbe Branch Account N° 31/00/6913072.

I do hope little or no inconvenience would arise from those operations being effected.

Thank you very much for your comprehension and cooperation.

Sincerely yours, P.A. Fossungu.

entail writing a voluminous book within this book. I can simply get you easily into what I am saying through a few of their fruitful *'Thank Yous'*. As some gifts theorists have counselled, a very genuine thank you for anything you receive from someone can work magic in doing away with obstacles that are standing in your way. "Always be grateful and thankful from the bottom of your heart therefore for every act of help that comes your way. It is because of this mannerism that I was able, for instance, to make the discovery regarding the BIROCOL money affair; and also able to extricate myself from the Takum (Nigeria) dire straits" (Fossungu, 2013c: 167). CGAMers really seem to have grasped this message like no other group of persons I know and I must make it clear that when it comes to appreciating and thanking for service rendered and received, CGAMers have almost no parallel. Just get what I mean from the few examples from the science of *thankyouology* that follow.

On July 10, 2006, James Tambong told 'Dear Goodwillers' how "My Family and myself are thankful to all Goodwillers for their visit to Gatineau. We are always delightful when Godwillers make this trip. This galvanizes our togetherness and demonstrates a very progressive and successful Goodwill Association. We hope you enjoyed the night in Gatineau. You all are always welcomed to Gatineau. See you soon. Thanks Again. James, Emilia, Kingsley, Yvonne, Melanie and Nicole [in] Gatineau" (paragraphing altered).[33] It must be indicated also that the very next day

---

[33] On July 11, 2006 Secretary-General Ibeagha responded for CGAM: Hi James, Hello Emilia: We also thank you for the successful hosting of the July Goodwill meeting. It was awesome and we had a nice time with you all. We also thank God for journey mercies as we arrived

after another return from Gatineau the president had (on August 14, 2005) extended thanks to the hosts and CGAMers. "On behalf of the Goodwill family, I would like to extend our appreciation and thanks to the Tambong family in Gatineau for the red carpet reception reserved for us all yesterday. As our Goodwill ambassadors to Ottawa, you make us proud whenever we make the trip there. Kudos to our DJs for the great animation. A great time was had by all. Congratulations also to all Goodwillers for the great turnout" (paragraphing altered).[34]

Mirabel Fambo Lukong in July 2006 invited the CGAM to their house-warming party in Châteauguay. Emmanuel Fokoua Tene (then Social Secretary) wrote back on July 8, 2006: *salut, à vous le plaisir fût le nôtre d'être spécialement invité par vous et nous apprécions à sa juste valeur ce geste de votre part. Bref nous vous félicitons de vos effort et demandons d'un seul coeur joyeux au seigneur de vous gardez dans son amour. Demeurer unis et restons goodwiller dans la joie et le malheur. Bien à vous* [paragraphing altered, and a few capitals added]. Yes indeed, Tene is very

---

safely back to base-Montreal and also all Goodwillers at home and abroad for all the prayers too. I wish you for and on behalf of Goodwill all the very best in the future. Warm regards [altered paragraphing].

[34] After the helpful counsel he received, relating to the insolent letter from NNA, Momany's dad also wrote to "My dear son" on February 7, 1999:

I have to thank you much for the two hundred US Dollars, which was 120.000 frs. When I was reading your letter it was you standing before me. I only pray to Almighty God [to] bless [us] to see each other. I thank you for all the advice you gave me about Njomo's letter.

Justine has [not] done well in this first term examination. She has only 7.9 average, but all the other terms she has been doing well. Many greetings from all the family people to you and [I] pray that God should keep you well until we meet. Thank you again for [the] money. Live well till we meet.

Your loving father, Fosungu N. Emmanuel.

right. The bond or solidarity of CGAMers is always there, whether it shines or rains. This *thankyouologistic* discussion can clearly not leave the stage without Vivian Beng's appreciation after the *cry-die* of her mother (at the Salle Marquette on 663, 2nd Avenue, Lachine) on June 24, 2006, with Goodwill's own DJ Alino mixing the 'juicy' ambience.[35] In *'THANKS AND THANKS AGAIN'* on June 29, 2006, Vivian wrote: "DEAR BROTHERS AND SISTERS OF THE GOODWILL [ASSOCIATION]: I wish to appreciate the presence of those Goodwillers who made me proud last Saturday by coming out to sit together and remember our Dear Mom once more. It was a great success because of all of you and the other well-wishers who came from far and near. Special thanks to those who sacrificed their time to put in extra efforts before and after the events. Thanks once again." There have obviously been so many of these crippling events in the community, it being especially hard on CGAMers when a member him/herself dies right here in town – as was the case in 2008 with Chris Ntongho, and others that would be canvassed in part three below. But I would not like to wrap up the classical *thankyouologists* with deaths, preferring to instead do so with the opposite (births).

---

[35] On June 15, 2006 DJ Alino (Alain Kamga Foko), obviously in response to Vivi's request, had written: "Hi Vivi: I wish you will rapidly forget the loss and think about the great day you will see each other ... I cannot refuse anything to you. I am ready to provide a juicy music for the occasion. If we need a professional set, let me know as soon as possible. I will surely play for fun, but the set is not for free. Please call me back and we will discuss... Have a nice day Vivi. DJ Alino mix [paragraphing changed]" When Alain talks of providing *a juicy music*, you should bear with him, as a French-speaker refusing to let language limit him. As usual, Peter A. Fossungu 'surprised' Vivian by immortalizing (video-taping) the event for her and other family members back home.

After the Goodwill community honoured their invitation to the birthday party of their daughter on Saturday July 22, 2006, the family head, Fidelis Folefac, classically wrote this *thankyouologistic* message on July 24, 2006:

Dear Friends and Goodwill members: We, The Folifacs, cannot afford to wait for the dust to settle before expressing our sincere gratitude for making the birthday party (July 22) of our youngest family member, Pearl, a befitting one. Your comportment, especially during the musical equipment Walhalla, was testimony of the fact [that] you were far from being a crowd but committed to providing us a useful company as usual. On behalf of my family, please do accept our thanks (I wish there was a better word other than thanks) for your time, moral and material support, no matter how small you think it was. Some of you came with friends whom we may not be able to reach through this forum or by phone, please do us the favor to extend our appreciation to them.

I am convinced that if our little girl could talk, she would have loved to hug all the kids who sang her first ever birthday song. The color and diversity they brought into the whole show was just amazing. Could Parents kindly, on behalf of Pearl, give these kids a special hug? Thank you for that.

For those who were unavoidabl[y] absent, we are equally thankful for your thoughts, inputs and concern. We could feel your spiritual presence and trust me Pearl did also.

We dove our hats to you all and pray for better days ahead, a more interactive and productive network. May the Almighty['s] fountain of blessings pour continuously on you and your family.

Useful Lessons and Excellent Comforters

Stifling deaths within the African community have obviously also furnished some very useful lessons, some of which came from the death of a Cameroonian in Montreal in September 2005. You get some of these 'Useful Lessons' from the CGAM president's message of September 28, 2005:

> I will like to take this opportunity to repeat a point I made during the meeting. As you know, a Cameroonian passed away in his sleep recently and it took three weeks for us to trace his family since the police took away his cell phone, address book and sealed his room. He had many friends, but none of them had any information on how to reach his family. I believe that Goodwillers can learn from this incident and take certain precautions JUST IN CASE:
>
> 1. Make sure your close friends have the phone number or e-mail address of one of your close family members who should be contacted in case of an emergency.
>
> 2. Make sure your family members back home or elsewhere have the phone number and e-mail address of your close friends here that they can contact in case of an emergency if they cannot reach you.
>
> 3. INSURANCE, INSURANCE, INSURANCE. Make sure you have even basic insurance and let your friends know that you have it. Also provide details of the insurance to your family back home: insurer, policy

number, insured amount and beneficiary. It serves no purpose to have insurance when no one knows about it (capitals are original).

Africans are not only classical *thankyouologists* but also excellent comforters of the grieving. It is obvious that a grieving person is more than grieving if no one is even around to say *Ashia*. That may largely explain why some critics have predicted "that socialism is the only practical alternative to contemporary capitalism. Teach them then what Africa has to offer in the field because it is all about money to these white people" (Fossungu, 2015a: 109). Learning of the loss of a daughter in Britain by a schoolmate of his, Peter A. Fossungu sent this condolence message to Thomas Ngembu on March 23, 2015 at 11.04 AM: "It is with a very heavy heart that I write to extend my sympathy for the loss of your beloved daughter. Words just cannot be enough and I wish distance didn't prevent us from being physically by your side during this extreme moment of grief to help you out. My wish however is that you continue to be strong since her other siblings and mum need you as their pillar of force at this moment more than most others. Take heart brother." Five minutes later Ngembu responded with: "You said it like you mean it and I could do with you my brothers around right now but I understand. Your words are golden to me right now and well appreciated. Thank you so very much and stay happy with yours and peace should reign."

Still on long-distance condolences, on June 7, 2006 Emmanuel Ngwakongnwi wrote from Thunder Bay (Ontario) to "Dear Hans, Karen, and Jackson" who were grieving, as follows:

It is heart breaking when we lose our relatives regardless of age or circumstance. Most of us have experienced this and I can understand how difficult this moment is for you all. Sometimes, you ask questions and may even be tempted to curse GOD. Never yield to this. I pray that you remain strong and be comforted by the word of God. For the bible says that there is time for everything. As we go through this cycle in life, I invite you to take courage with the words of Joseph Scrivens. This is a man who lost the wife on the day of their wedding, but could do nothing than being inspired to write one of today's most famous Hymns. 'What a friend we have in Jesus'. Once more be courageous and extend my condolences to your entire family.[36]

Challenging as the grief of members who lose loved ones may be, CGAMers have had to confront even more Herculean challenges and controversies when it has been the death of a CGAMer him or herself, the more so when the

---

[36] On June 8, 2006, Adolf Achu Ammah sent this interesting sympathy message to Jackson Acha Atam who lost his aunty: "Hi Jackson: How are you today? When I learned of the dead [sic] of your only aunt I sympathised with you initially. After careful meditation and profound deliberations, and after thinking of what Jesus told Martha and Mary when they lost their only brother Lazarus, I withdrew all my sympathy. Jesus told them *'I am the resurrection and the life; he who believe in me, though he die, yet he shall live, and whoever lives and believe in me shall never die'*. Jackson, Remember that God created man according to his own image and we all carry a sign he implanted in us. Have you ever thought of the fact that when you stretch out both of your hands you form a big cross? Do you know that you also carry a cross on your face? That is a sign that we are in God and he is in us. So he is in total control of our lives and whatever is happening to us. Remember he knows the past, present, future and he knows what is good for us. He uses life's reverses to push us ahead. We don't live to design tomorrow but to discover it, since God designed it since when we were in our mother's womb. .... Cheer up brother and continue to keep the faith." [Omission and italics are original]

member dies in town (as was the case of Chris Ntongho) or out-of-town (like Georges Neba and Vivian Beng). But as much as these tragedies should be points of unity, they can be counter-productive to the unity cause when rules in their regard are not applied without letting personal emotions and attachments take the centre stage. Material from previous sections acquaints you with some of the deaths we are discussing, a debate that will continue with (1) the democracy debate on the death social package, leading to the hijacking of the Brother/Sister relationship out of the covered domain, and (2) dealing with member deaths.

Death *Sociopackism* Compensation Rules and Visionlessness: Hijacking Brosisterism and the IUIU Constitutional Obligation

The Social Package on Death could not have been an exception to the general review that took place in the CGAM January 2006 Assembly, through the Najemehist Bylaws Revision Committee (BRC). A proposal on the issue was that the $400.00 earmarked for bereavement should be limited to parents, spouses, children and siblings. A definition of sibling was advanced by the BRC chairman (Hans Najeme) as including blood relations e.g. direct brothers/sisters and step brothers/sisters. A contrary opinion came from the president (Paul Ayah) who said that it is difficult to define siblings to encompass so many different blood lines and besides, that there was need to increase the amount of members' contribution to the fund for the smooth running of the association. The visionless nature of these two issues will be elaborated on under (1) What Shall I Call Them (in the next chapter) and (2) Need for Increased Contribution.

Hijacking *Brosisterism* and the Question of Death Contributions Augmentation

Hans Najeme said there was no need for an increment of the emergency fund contributions. Rather, he suggested, members should be called upon to contribute towards an event if the fund is depleted. Secretary-General Aloysius Ibeagha was of the opinion that there need to be a balance in that when funds are depleted, members should contribute to the fund. The Goodwill General Assembly (GGA) agreed not to raise contributions to the emergency fund and agreed that members will contribute towards an event if the emergency fund is depleted. Visionlessness, you can begin to say. Fidelis Follifac (also a member of that BRC) called for the adoption of the definition of sibling, which was duly adopted. Now, I am sure that I see *visionlessness* here, if no one else does. What do you also see? *Charalicing* opportunists too, you would say? Why all these questions? Because you would have thought that this matter was already shut out till the next "Yearly Bylaws Revision".

Not so when you are dealing with schemers and tree-toppers or *viperizationised charalicers*. Thus, we would be back on the death palaver again just two months later. At the March 2006 GGA, the discussion on death resurfaced and raged on as follows:

Fidelis Follifac made an observation concerning article 5 of the bylaws which stipulates that two third members of the general assembly could suspend the constitution to enable it deliberate and adopt new laws. This he further explained was concerning giving $400.00 dollars to a bereaved member which he considered a small amount, giving of a purse ($200.00) to a member who is getting married (or engaged?) and modalities of leaving the association. These issues were either not clearly stated/covered by the bylaws or needed revisiting. The president apologized on behalf of the association for giving a purse to a member who was getting engaged and explained that we w[]ere all carried by the joy of the occasion. He said the bylaws will be followed strictly in the future. On the issue of leaving the association, the president said that any member wanting to leave the association would be asked to write and sign a document to that effect. On giving to the bereaved, the president said that $400.00 was just a token and not meant to fund a burial. A heated debate followed this and the President closed the topic by saying that suspending the constitution to allow discussions on these issues was not possible because only an "extraordinary" issue can lead to the suspension of the constitution.

Forty one members attended the March meeting.

The meeting ended at 11.10 pm followed by dancing, dancing, dancing (GGA Minutes of March 2006)

But the tree-toppers would no longer have any sleep, using the nights to concoct every strategy imaginable to oust the *Paulayahist* government, and making sure to enlist or recruit enough cronies for the (motion-majority-vote) plot. Anyone doubting what I am saying could, for example, consult the May 2006 GGA, where 'the Adoption of minutes of April meeting' would make the point very well: "The minutes of the last meeting was read out by the Secretary General. Fidelis Folifac observed that the minutes were well taken but that it did not mention the attempted resignation by the Secretary General. The Sec. Gen. responded by saying that his attempt at resigning was not an extraordinary issue (laughter on the floor). The President added that it was rejected by both the executive committee and the General Assembly." A further discussion of this Minutes-Taking Fiasco can be pursued in Fossungu (2015b: 128-136).

The truncated April minutes would say at the end that the President finally craved the indulgence of the house to tackle the issue in the next [May] meeting. But I think the *president* being referred to here could be that of the *midnighters*, not the one officially known to CGAM. The CGAM president rather said this issue was closed in the last meeting (March) and that we had just been wasting time that April evening, indicating that we did not then have any more time for the other items on the agenda since the presenter for that evening (from the embassy in Ottawa) was there and ready to deliver. It is therefore those other issues not discussed and not this closed 'extraordinary death issue' that were to be discussed in the following [May] meeting. As the discussion of *postponementolodrama* has shown (see Fossungu, 2015b: chapter 4), the *midnighters* never went to sleep over the issue of unseating the president by whatever means.

The CGAM April 2006 buffet opened very 'extraordinarily' late before the presentation of the High Commissioner's representative, which I would not want to go into here. The important thing to note is that the Battle of Death had been lost that evening but not the war which you could clearly see continuing in the *August Democracy Hall* (better known as *postponementolodrama*) and up to when Mr. Hardliner unwittingly helped one of the hijackers to hijack his fellow hijackers, as seen in Fossungu (2015b: chapter 3). Following that hijacker hijacking, will be the hijacking of brothers and sisters (*brosisterism*) for strangers. Was brosisterism not hijacked by strangers in the CGAM? Some would answer in the affirmative while others in the negative. But I would like you to listen to the essential parts of the Minutes of July 2007 GGA and be the sapient judge:

Born Houses and Death

The president welcomes the newly born baby to the family of Ntongho Chrisantus and handed a check of 350$ to the family as Goodwill's gesture. He also handed out two other checks (200$ each) to the families of Ako-Arrey Denis and Ammah for the birth of babies into their families sometimes last year. Fambo Mirabel during this meeting announced the born house of their son to be in the third weekend of August (Saturday the 18th).

The president also handed a check of 1500$ to the family of Dr. Peter Fossungu as Goodwill's contributions to the death of his younger brother in June this year.

Some members asked why the executive did not take prompt action concerning the handing of the check to Dr. Peter Fossungu immediately when he lost his brother. The president told the assembly that the incident coincided with the death of Evodia's sister towards which members were making contributions and there was no money in the account of the association for any quick action since the association depends on members' contribution to resolve such issues. ....

Another issue that was highly debated by the assembly was that of members' contributing towards the death of Tatuh Felicia's step brother who died sometimes in April this year. Some members argued that Felicia did not inform the Goodwill community on time and/or the executive of the association of her loss. So they do not see the importance of the loss to her and found it unrealistic to make contributions towards the death which was already two months old. Others argued that the few members she informed ought to have informed the Goodwill community of her loss to enable others to sympathize with her while she herself said she was not aware that the association makes contributions towards the loss of a brother.

Goodwill's executive on her part argued that the death was learnt of after two months and its position is to bring the issue to the assembly for a decision. The matter was put to vote and 12 members voted to make contribution towards the death while 18 members voted against. The assembly then adopted that henceforth if a member has a problem, he/she has 48 hours to report the matter to Goodwill's executive to make it official.

Revisit of Bylaws

Following the heated arguments in regards to contributions towards the death of Felicia's step brother, the executive proposed the revisit of the bylaws particularly the clause on deaths. This clause was revisited by the general assembly and concluded that henceforth contributions towards death will be as follows:

1) 1500$ for the death of a member's father or mother

2) 1500$ for the death of a biological or legally adopted kid in Canada of a member

3) 1500$ for the death of a legal husband or spouse of a member

4) No contributions towards the death of a brother or sister of a member

Dealing with Death of a Member (CGAMer): The IUIU Constitutional Obligation

IUIU, for those who want it in a hurry, means 'Indirect, Unclean, Inexplicable and Unclear'. Fossungu (2015b: chapter 4) has already extensively handled the adhocist and controversial scrapping of the above-cited category-4 deaths in the 'Revisit of Bylaws' outlined above. There is no better way to fortify your understanding of the Deceptive Battle of Death here than through the examination of the cases with an indirect, unclean, inexplicable and unclear constitutional obligation. I am referring to the death of a CGAMer. Well, those who say Momany was talking from the viewpoint of 'someone guilty of having taken our cheque for the death of a brother that was not in fact a brother' (see Fossungu, 2015b: 106-115) would have to also explain to you if Momany had also died (like Chris, Georges, and Vivian) and then defied Fon DF Fossungu's thesis by coming back to speak for himself. Let us examine these three cases, one of which is in-town with the others being out-of-town.

The Ntongho File: What Constitutional Base Has the In-Town Story?

The question is graphical because the Chris Ntongho case quickly brings 99-sensism to mind, when the circumstances are carefully examined. Remember too that the July 2007 Assembly's Bylaw-Revisit reiterated also that there is to be payment of "1500$ for the death of a legal husband or spouse of a member". The dead member him or herself is not covered: hence the inexplicability in the IUIU. Why I should be financially helped when I have lost someone but not when

I lost my own life, may seem awkward at first glance, but not so on closer inspection. First, the help is meant for aiding the living member cope with the death of those covered. Second, death ends one's membership and constitutional rights and obligation of CGAM. Assuming that Ntongho's wife was a member, logic would suggest that the family receives in total $1500.00 because only the living member spouse is covered, not the dead member. As I have said, it looks strange but that is the correct reading of the 'Revisit of Bylaws' category-3 deaths, with none of the categories covering the dead member.

But let's suppose now that both living spouse and dead partner are covered in category-3: the family gets a total of $3000.00 ($1500 for the living spouse member plus $1500.00 for the dead member). That was just a supposition. Only one part of our assumption applies in the law just noted though, limiting the CGAM package to $1500.00. Chris Ntongho's case is not even covered by that one-half. The Mungwa File of 2007 even had less controversy, put alongside Ntongho's because, although the deceased was not a CGAMer, her sister was. CGAM owed the sister no financial obligation since *brosisterism* had been scrapped. But the fact that the deceased's sister and brother-in-law were CGAMers could make a difference. We could assume that CGAMers were there aiding one or two of *their members*. On the contrary, Mrs. Ntongho was present in Montreal, but was never a CGAMer, making absolutely no sense (absent 99-sensism) why CGAM would be doing all what it actually did.

This is what instead actually happened. Ntongho joined the CGAM in January 2007, having been sponsored by no other than the tree-topperism high priest, Fidelis Folefac. Ntongho's wife never came into CGAM with him. At the famous brosisterism-hijacking July 2007 session, you have noted that Ntongho also received the birth cheque of $350 while others were receiving $200 for the same births, why? At the same session, Secretary-General Jackson Acha Atam was not amused because some members "were curious about the fact that Ntongho Chrisantus['] illness [cancer] was not reported to the Goodwill's community. The S.G of Goodwill told the assembly that the family of Mr. Ntongho opted to keep the illness private and that a similar incident occurred sometime this year and was made public by the office of the S.G in good faith but those concern[ed] did not appreciate it." Wouldn't it have been amazing to you if tree-toppers and *doublesidists* appreciate such truth?

If you are neither of those exploitative pretenders, there will be no reason or need for fearing people around you knowing the truth about you or what you do or are planning to do. With this theory adequately grasped, you would not then be very surprised by attitudes such as Scholastica's when she reaches NNA, and precisely Canada. You could quickly see what I am saying especially from her letter of May 19, 1996 to her husband in which she wrote:

> Power! I presume you are writing your exams well. Let's pray that God should give you a small job when you are through with your course. That is my greatest wish every day. Power, you need to renew your visa.
>
> Power, don't you see with me that Elias should not be aware of my coming to meet you now? I thought of it only yesterday. He may hear this and decide not to give me anything again. Also, he will tell his wife and some people and they would [have] many stories to make. Please, you can write and tell him that I used to complain

of my stomach a lot. That he can help and give me money so that I use in taking treatment where the wife of Michael Akendung was. These will already be my preparation of coming. For the passport, it is not difficult when there is money. We can always make it even in one week. Please, do not tell Elias. You can explain as I have said and he should be aware only about one month to my coming, i.e., when we are already sure.

Since Pa has been complaining a lot about his money, you can write and tell them only about one month [to] go. Telling them that it is a scholarship opportunity for the wives of those studying there so that they can come together or anything, but it should not be that you would be the one to take charge. Please, that is the only way you can tell them because people will make a lot of noise, that you took people's money and is [sic] now calling for your wife without refunding them. Pa went to Limbe to collect his money, and they told him to come only in July [1996], that the money will be unlocked only in July because you can still need money and ask them to send it. Pa came back and grumbled the whole day as I heard. Anyway, after everything he said he damned the consequences if it is because of Peter.

Power, you can also try to contact some white friends or it may be Nancy's family that they should be the ones to invite me. If not so, they wouldn't give me a visa here. It is very difficult to give visas now. Most people use but this trick. Anyway we shall discuss better when the time comes.

I went and asked about the transcript and they said it can be given at the end of two semesters if you apply with some money. An attestation can also be given.

Power, my dad is still here and will be going to Douala tomorrow. I am writing this letter so that he can take it to Brother Romanus to post for me. I have a test tomorrow. It is 2 a.m. and I am feeling sleepy. I shall write more only next time. I am sure you must have seen my first letter.

Steve and Jess wrote to me acknowledging the recei[pt] of your letter. They also sent 2000 francs to me through my father. The money will really help me. I don't go to Douala often because of high transport and lack of time.

Power, I shall still write in two weeks' time. I don't know if by then I will [sic] have received a letter from you, I shall call also.

I miss you, and will be more than the word happy if things should move the way you want. All this time I pray that God should make things to move for us, for we miss each other a lot. I also imagine how our face [first?] meeting will look like; it may be at the airport when you will come to collect me.

Love. Schola

The questions to pose are many but just use these few and extrapolate, if you will. Scholastica talks too much about 'the stories' to be made regarding people's monies if Power's plans of bringing her to NNA are known to Power's family members (who, by the way, do not even respond to his letters). But why wouldn't she fervently work in helping the same Power to repay those debts when she eventually crosses over two years later? What could 'the many stories' (that she was so afraid of) then really be about? 99-sensism is in place here as was in the Chris Ntongho File, yes or no? If you are still wondering what to select for an answer then read on and dissipate your doubts. At the April 2009 Assembly, there was an item known as "Reflection on Chris' Funeral". The president, Fidelis Folefac, it tells us,

> opened the page with words of gratitude expressed by the Ntongho family to Goodwill. He termed this occurrence a trial moment for Goodwill; for it was the first time, an active member lost their lives. He congratulated members on their spontaneous response to the demanding tasks that were asked of them during that period. Furthermore, he asked members to reflect on the positive as well as the negative aspects of the celebration, to retain what was done correctly and to ameliorate on those that needed more efforts, subsequently.
>
> The flo[or was] flooded with opinions; recurrent was congratulatory and the acquisition of a life insurance plan by each Goodwill member. All who commented on this aspect congratulated the current Executive and particularly the President for his ingenuity that led to the success of that celebration. More importantly, all speakers advised members to acquire an Insurance plan for their families. The importance of this advice was heightened when the President in closing remarks on this point, gave the last words of Chris to members, "whoever comes to Canada should acquire an Insurance plan as soon as they set their feet in Canada. They should not wait until they become ill to seek insurance." To round it off, he gave the Assembly a recapitulation of how the money donated was used:
>
> $2400 was spent for the funeral home,

$2500 was given to support the funeral expenses in Cameroon,

$2000 was given to Chris' mum

$3000 was given to the widow for use in Cameroon

The balance [of how much?] was to be transferred to the Ntongho Family account for his widow and children's support.

There is obviously a lot more that can be said about this file, but this much tells you what Goodwillers, led by their leaders would do to manage deaths within their community. The big fat question that arises here and there is one of consistency in dealing with the cases. Specifically: are the cases handled fairly or are some considered more important than others, depending on who is president and what their personal relationships with the affected are?

The *Outstationistic* Beng-Neba Files: Hiding Something Behind Deaths?

This question may seem surprising but it is in place. Amazing because many would not fathom any right-thinking person choosing death as a hiding place, right? But is the world made up of only the right-thinking? Not to plunge you into the philosophy of death that members of my large family are expert at, you remember hearing above that death may provoke the worst in some family members? Yes. That could be true but sometimes death does only provide a hiding platform for what has always been there to be vented. Just listen to Joseph's other letter to his father to better assimilate the point. This letter too is undated but was surely written before his mother's death that purportedly provoked the other *josephizationing* letter you have already read above. The present letter (which, at least, bears his Dallas, Texas postal contact and full name) runs thus:

My dear Father: This is to let you understand that I am seek [sic] of writing [to] you without hearing from you for a long time. You know what? I don't think you are a child and you shouldn't act like one. Whenever I send you a letter, I think [you] should reply.

You know what? I have finally decided to end the business deal I was trying to do with you, because you are not good. Your mind has been poisoned by the Fosungu family and your ugly Balondo woman.

Tell Richard in Douala that I say I don't like all of them. In short, I hate your Fosungu Family. You are not a chief because you let people advise you instead of you advising them. Richard is a thief who wanted me to send him cars to put on the streets as taxi and failed to tell me you were trying to buy a bus and give [to] him.

I am seek [sic] of you all including my mother who has never written to me since I have been in the U.S.A. Your close friends are all prostitutes. I mean your Chaterine [sic] and Theresia. You know what? Even if you hear Joe Fosungu is dead, don't cry. You have kept a lot of secrets from me. I think you are insane. Your Balondo stupid woman has poisoned your mind to the exten[t] that you have abandoned the only child you are proud of. Shame unto you!

Don't write [to] me no more unless you are ready to apologize for your actions. I am not a small child. I have decided to take U.S. citizenship and I am going to come home and marry my sweet heart who is in Yaoundé called

Gladys. Don't write me I repeat; and make sure you let your stupid Fosungu people read this letter. Also let the chief read this letter. I thought I could work with you and make the family better, but you are not good. If you write me without apologizing, I will send your letter back to you. I am serious. My decision includes my mother. Do you understand? Bye.

The Nwangong Royal Family Politics can be so complexly informative, hurtful and enjoyable – all at once. That, I think, is the logical price and beauty of multitude and diversity: the more interestingly so when truthfully exposed. Of course, I need not repeat here that truthful is objective and also that Joseph Njumo Fosungu is not wrong or alone on the question of not having his father's replies to his letters. It is not just Joe who has that issue going. We also hear one of his brothers saying the same thing on August 3, 1998, albeit in quite a very different tone:

Dear father: I was shocked to hear that you never received the letter (a copy of which is here enclosed) that I sent through the [Muyuka] Catholic Mission address after hearing of the death that occurred. Even more shocking to me is the fact that you could even think that I never wrote, when I will be the one who gave the address to Marie-Claire. It really seems to me that no one in this world actually understands who I am.

Well, I am sure my letter (which was sent long before Marie's) never got to you because of the $100 US dollars that I managed to put inside in the form of travellers' cheques. The problem now is not even so much that money. But I think I should have understood what had happened to the letter in time if my letters were usually acknowledged. I am not now talking about your case; but I really don't know what to say because, since I got here I have written to several members of this family and never, until this moment, got any signs that my letters were ever received.

Even when I talked to Mr. Elias some time before they (in Douala) were coming to see you, I was wondering if you have got that fateful letter. I wonder if he never brushed this issue with you while they were there. It is now quite clear to me that should Scholastica no longer be there I will never know anything that is happening to the family back there. Whether it is good or bad news, no one ever bothers to let me know.

Why then do I always indicate my phone number in letters? It is not for fancy, or that people should always call me. The essence of it is for cases like the death that just occurred. In such circumstances, you people can always get to any phone booth and just call me and give me the number of the place and I call back to be told whatever it is.

It should be noted that my address has changed since the May letter. And, that nothing is enclosed here as indicated in that May letter. It is just an unsigned copy of the original letter I sent long ago. I just thought I should print a copy now and enclose here.

Extend my greetings to everyone. Sincerely, P.A. Fossungu.

I am sure that Momany got a response from his father on November 6, 1998 because he never placed any interdiction on or conditions of a reply.[37] Talking about deaths in the family that are not well reported and/or taken care of would squarely bring the **Vivian-Beng File** to mind. On Friday, December 18, 2009 at 4.04 PM, Fidelis Folefac, as CGAM president, forwarded this message from Sylvanus Asonganyi,[38] with this note of his own:

---

[37] The father's November 6, 1998 Letter to "Dear Son" reads:

I saw your letters to me but it is because of ill-health that you cannot have my reply in time, especially the one concerning the death of my late wife Mrs. Thecla Anangafac. You should know that there is no telephone in the whole of Muyuka Sub Division. Here is a copy of an insulti[ng] letter to me from my own son, Njumo Joseph, in USA concerning the death of his late mother. I wish you should read it cautiously and give me your own advice. Your brother Fosungu Valentine died in a motor accident on the 25th October 1998 in Malende Village (Muyuka Sub-Division). His corpse was carr[ied] to the village (Nwangong) where the burial took place. When do you expect to come to Cameroon again? If you have known try to tell me in your next letter to me.

Mbancho Bernard is now in South Africa in search of a job opportunity there.

You are warmly accorded greetings from the entire family.

Papa Emmanuel N. Fosungu

[38] PLEASE CIRCULATE WIDELY

Dear brothers and sisters

On behalf of the Cameroonian Community in Calgary – Canada, I announce with a very heavy heart, the transition onto the Lord of ... our sister, aunt and mother Miss. Vivian Sih Beng.

She passed away [y]esterday Thursday December 17th, 2009 at about 2:45 am at the University of Calgary Foothills Hospital after a protracted illness.

Vivian was born in Wum, Northwest province of Cameroon on October 16, 1971. She graduated from the University of Buea in 1998, moved to Europe a few years afterwards before relocating to Montreal Canada in 2001. She graduated with a BA in Sociology from the University of McGill in 2008 before moving to [C]algary that same year. In Sept. 2009, she got admission into the faculty of Social Works - University of Calgary where she studied until her time of death.

She leaves behind in Canada two daughters Melanie (17) and Lisa (8), [h]er Aunt (currently visiting her in Calgary), 4 siblings, lots of friends,

"Dear All, See message below from Chief Asonganyi from Calgary. May I add that Vivian was a founding member of Goodwill and a member until her relocation to Calgary. May her [soul] rest in perfect peace. Fidelis [paragraphing altered]" I must indicate here that Sylvanus Asonganyi had also been a CGAMer who relocated to Calgary like the deceased.

Magnus Ajong reacted the same day (December 18) at 12.20 PM when he wrote: "President, Thanks for circulating the program. May I ask what is Goodwill's position as per the

---

relatives and world [sic] wishers to mourn her. In order to give Vivian a befitting last respect that reflects her wishes, a fund-raising drive has been launched to assist the family with the pre and post funeral logistics both in Canada and at her final resting place in Cameroon.

Below is the bank information for your generous support:
MEMO:
Vivian's Memorial Fund
PAYABLE TO: Mrs Rosaline Fogwe
BANK NAME: TD Canada Trust
BRANCH#: 004
ACCOUNT #: 7567 6519347
TRANSIT #: 01729
Swift Code (for international wiring) : TDOMCATTTOR
4415 Memorial Dr. SE
Calgary, Alberta
T2A 6A4

E-mail money transfers should be directed to rfongwe@yahoo. Com We will like to acknowledge all contributions, as such, it will be appreciated if you would include your contact information with your transaction. For all those who are will[ing] to contribute but can't make it to any financial institution, please contact the following friends and relatives to hand in any generous donations.

Fung George (Ottawa) Telephone: (613)... [XXX- YYYY] Gerald Wallang (Montreal): Telephone: (514)... [YYY-XXXX] Wake-keep information will be communicated later. For any other general inquiries please call chief (403)... [XXX-YYYY] May God Bless us all.

Vivian , u will 4 ever be missed. Chief Asonganyi On behalf of the Cameroon Community in Calgary.

assistance of the corpse's repatriation? My suggestion is that goodwillers can chip in their contribution to a single contact person which can then be forwarded to Calgary as a lump sum – just a suggestion though. Kind regards." Fidelis Folefac then responded on same December 18:

Dear Dr. Ajong,

Thanks for this important question. I will be contributing as an individual (Fidelis Folifac) and encourage EVERY Goodwiller to do so if deemed necessary.

On Goodwill's position, as per our constitution and by-laws we have no obligation to past members. Remember that we had a similar case last year (Neba George-RIP) and we did not do anything as Goodwill. It is my conviction that it is important for us [in] an association not to give the impression that we handle issues based on who is concern[ed].

However, when Goodwill was bereaved [Ntongho's case, he means], I sent a customized email to the presidents of MECA Toronto, K-Towners, G12, Ottawa Njangi and other associations requesting for assistance. They came to our assistance and we did recognize[] that. Thus if we were to receive a customized email addressed to Goodwill, we would set up a collection unit, and I will make my contribution through Goodwill. Any amount collected will be forwarded as generous support from Goodwill without the names of the individuals. The list of contributors will only be published within Goodwill.

As the team in Calgary is in constant touch with me to get tips on how we handled our [Chris Ntongho] case, I have shared this information with them.

Hope this provides some clarifications.
Best regards. Fidelis

The Neba File: Yes, of course, Mr. President. I wouldn't need to go into the details of the Neba case here since the president has also covered it: Zero action. So, the non-member death in Montreal (see Fossungu, 2015b: 106-120) requested a "customized email" to Goodwill president who caused Goodwill to assume complete responsibility? I would need only to reiterate, first, that Ntongho's case was not constitutionally covered (as demonstrated above). Second, that Georges died in 2009 (January) and not in 2008 (last year, as the president says). By the way, 2008 was a year still under the presidency of Fidelis Folefac. And, third, that Georges died in an accident in Cameroon while visiting from Germany where he was working but still based in Montreal – his wife and child and mother-in-law being in LaSalle, the seat of the CGAM. On January 21, 2009 the headline was '*A Former Goodwiller Is Gone*' when Jules Komguep announced to 'Fellow Goodwillers' that:

> This is to let you know that one of our former member[
> GEORGE NEBA died last Sunday January 19th in Cameroo
> in a motor accident on Douala-Limbe roa
> George Neba and the wife Christine were active members o
> Goodwill in 2005 and 2006, before George moved
> Germany where he had a job. During his membership i
> Goodwill, he participated in many committees (Goodw
> project committee and Constitution and Bylaws Committe
> and activities. He also used to come and support Goodw
> FC   soccer   matche
> The bereaved family (Christine and the daughter Mea) can k

112

reached at this number 514-[XXX-YYYY].

Let us have a minute of prayer for his soul to rest in peace.

Find attached some of his pictures.

The following day (January 22), the Ibeaghas (one of the principal family organizers of *the 2007 non-member Goodwill-assumed death*[39]) addressed 'Dear All' and offered "Our

---

[39] Hans Najeme, who would now quickly come down from the tree-top because of the case we are now talking about, provided us with the *'Final Funeral Statement'* when on November 7, 2007 he made the following known to 'Fellow Goodwillers':

Below is a summary of the final report on the Stephania Fund drive. All amounts in Canadian dolars, as presented by Mrs Ibeagha.

Summary Income

Goodwill	4865
Cameroonians in Montreal and Canada	1747
Non Cameroonians in Montreal	320
Cameroonians in USA	600
Family Members Europe	2749
Family Members USA	2530
Total 12811	

Expenditure	Amount	Date
Payment to Funeral home	190 0	26.08. 2007
Drinks	200	08.09. 2007
Meat	100	08.09. 2007
Fruits	20	08.09. 2007
Chewables	50	08.09. 2007
Payment to Funeral home	360 0	08.09. 2007

			08.09.
Hall (Wake Keep)		120	2007
		100	12.09.
Payment to Funeral home	0		2007
Total 6990			

Cash at hand

Income – Expenditure 12811-6990 = 5821

Cash at hand of $5821.00 Can has been deposited into Goodwill account (see attached). The detailed report has been sent to the president. I am only sending a summary income to you for reasons that would be made known to you by the president. Any further enquiries concerning this issue should be addressed to the president as it is now officially out of my hands.

Please note that after the comity meeting that took place on Friday November 2nd, a cheque of $3353.63 was issued payable to the funeral home, a cheque for the balance ($2467.37), was issued to Mr. Peter Mungwa. Mr. and Mrs Mungwa brought to my attention, a money gram receipt of this entire balance sent to the deceased's father to use for the child left behind. They insist on assuring the community that the entire surplus from the fund raising has been sent to Cameroon for the up-keep of the child.

Once again thanks to all Goo[d]willers for your support and more importantly, our prayers for the berieved [sic] family. May God give them courage to move on and take care of the young child left behind.

Blessings to you all. In Goodwill. President

Michel Ntemgwa's sane question on this issue would simply receive total silence for an answer. On November 8, 2007 he wrote back:

I will like to first of all thank the committee for a job that was well executed and that by Gods grace we can say Goodwill, family members, Cameroonians who are not members of goodwill and even non-Cameroonians participated in this very difficult task. In regard to this email that was posted. I will like to know why it took the committee till November 2 to issue a $3353.63 cheque to the funeral home. Is it that they gave us a period of grace or that money that was collected was may be sometimes in the form of pledges that still had to be honored? The figures of income and expenditure add up very well above but when you add the $2467.37 and $3353.63 below it gives us 5821 what is said to have been deposited in goodwill account. Does this really mean the balance in goodwill account is zero? If so it could have been better to just put these two amounts as expenditure because the thoughts and prayers to the bereaved family. It is indeed a shock to hear that Georges Neba is no more. Very jovial, kind, friendly and a loving brother, dad, uncle and husband. Only God knows why He called him now. May his gentle soul rest in the bosom of the Lord. Accept our heart-felt condolences friends and family. Eveline and Aloy Ibeagha." The same day Martha Tanyi-Mbianyor wrote in her capacity as CGAM vice-president as follows:

Fellow Goodwillers, it is with deep sympathy to hear again death is around the corner. We always pray for things like this never to happen, but if it does, we take heart and pray for God's guidance and protection.

It is sad to lose a love[d] one especially someone we call our own like George Neba. He was a fully committed Goodwiller, so Goodwill is touched again by the cold hands of death. Whatever must have happened to him God knows why and best.

This is not the time to cry but to hold on to the Lord and be strong in him. He will wipe away our tears. So I call upon all to pray for his soul to rest in perfect peace and for the bereaved family (wife and kids) who are here in [M]ontreal I believe. Please, to remember our brother in the best possible way we can, I plead with members to find time and visit the family here in [M]ontreal or make a phone call to the family. In this way, George will tru[]ly know he had had a family in Montreal called Goodwill with love and care.

---

initial presentation makes us to believe there is balance when in fact there is none. May be I am wrong but a committee member should correct me on this.

Thanks

Michel

George may you rest in the bosom of the Lord Almigthy and may he grant you eternal rest in peace.

On behalf of my team, I express our deepest sympathy to the decease[d's] family at home and abroad.

Martha Tanyi-Mbianyor VP

There was clearly no CGAM president this time around because Fidelis Folefac on January 23, 2009 simply wrote on behalf of himself and his family as follows:

This is disgusting and devastating. No! no George, I wish someone can tell us that we are dreaming, or someone can tell us that this was just an expensive scam.

George was a true community person whose sense of commitment, brotherliness and understanding created a positive impact in many individual[s]. I can vividly remember working with this fine gentleman in the Goodwill Project Committee. His active participation in Goodwill F.C. and interaction in the community are so fresh in my mind.

My brother, what is this life all about? Nothingness, indeed, nothingness.

I trust that God has spoken and let is [sic] be so. We are comforted that this is a sure path for all and that in Him there is peace and everlasting joy.

May God provide His comfort, strength and blessings for the family and friends mourning your departure from this sinful world.

If anyone has further information on the funeral program please kindly communicate it to me.

George, go well and prepare a place for us till we meet to part no more.

May his soul rest in perfect peace.

God knows why
The Folifacs

I am not the one telling you that the CGAM did absolutely nothing. Yet, these same guys had the CGAM regular activities cancelled because of the death of a total stranger (non-member) whose corpse CGAM *freewilldonationly* did *everything* to ship to Cameroon (see Fossungu, 2015b: chapter 4). Now, let those CGAMers that *freewilldonationly* gave a hundred dollars to the Beng-Fund plea come forward and let us see them. There is clearly none of them. If you do not brand this *politickerization* gone wild in NNA, then give me another term for it, so that I could start employing but that new nomenclature to the birth-marriage versions that seriously would also call the validity of the GAC (if not CGAM itself) into multiple and endless questions.

Chapter 4

Africans Singing Family And *Trijuralism*: *Doublesidism* And The Birth-Marriage *Sociopackism* Politics

What western media generally failed to report, underreported, or conveyed in a distorted and strongly biased fashion was that: Laurent Gabgbo and his party had brought the case to the Supreme Court; that the Supreme Court of Ivory Coast had recounted the votes; that the Supreme Court had taken notice of election fraud in favor of Outtara; and that the Supreme Court of Ivory Coast had declared Laurent Gbagbo to be the winner of the elections and the rightfully elected President of Ivory Coast. That French backed guerrilla began attacking predominantly pro-Gbagbo villages, committing massacres, and that French backed "rebels" were attacking the Presidential Residence (Lehmann, 2007).

The chapter is in three parts. The first deals with marriage *trijuralism* and family relationship *oddifacism*. The next looks at the debt recovery fiasco in the context of the catch-all African umbrella. The last part examines the scrapping of birth-marriage *sociopackism*

Marriage *Trijuralism* and Relationship *Oddifacism:* *Marijamesing* the Police-Family Thesis and What Shall I Call Them?

The problems of marriage and family in Africa have preoccupied not only academicians of all hues. Cameroonian singers have also been very pronounced in the domain. For instance, in *Thunder* Petit-Pays (self-styled *l'avocat des femmes*) talks about some family members who are like the police: in the sense that they only take and take, never giving; with Fossungu (2013c & 2014) confirming to a large extent. The question boils down to whether or not Africans are Singing Marriage and Family in Cameroon and Muting It in Northern North America? A positive response would be advanced by the books just cited wherein you will learn of the Gift Theory, centred on the giver-receiver equation that police-like people destabilize all the time: thus redefining family relations in a way that leaves them always on the receiving end. But since we are now talking about marriage and family deceptive politics in NNA, it would be more appropriate to give you a localized case that also lingers on the confusion of Canada and the USA as a single country for the purpose of acquiring cheap popularity. I am talking about (1) *marijamesing* the police-family thesis and (2) *police-inspectorizing* the same police-family theory.

Marijamesing the Police-Family Thesis

These issues and more come out in Momany's extensive communication to "Dear Marie-Claire & James" on March 26, 1999:

I may not have this or that, that and this; but I have one thing that nobody, repeat and capitalize NOBODY, whomsoever can take away from me. I am talking about my DIGNITY.

What are these wild stories I hear you guys have been sending home? That I am living with you guys in the United States? That you guys are bringing my wife, Scholastica, to the United States? And many more, perhaps, that I am yet to hear of? Since when did 1830A Lincoln Avenue in Montreal, Quebec, Canada become 16403 Everwood Court in Bowie, Maryland, United States? I am really surprised by both of you, but you, Marie-Claire, in particular. I might have to pardon James for not knowing me; but should I do the same to you Marie-Claire?

I really begin to see why, some days to mum's arrival, you guys were talking on the phone about rents (It is even as if I asked you guys to pay my rents for me in the first place) I should be saving if I came down there. So you just wanted mum from Cameroon to get there and meet me at home with you and confirm these lies? Unfortunately, for you, I just happen not to be the type that was brought up to depend on people and, consequently, would quickly jump into such traps. Just to imagine that you even set up such ploys makes my stomach ache. What must you have told mum when she got there and there was no Peter? That I have just paid a brief visit to Canada? When was the first and last time I was at your residence?

I will tell you if you have forgotten. From 20 December 1997 to 22 January 1998. Actually, I am not suggesting that living with you guys is so wrong. But try not to go about boasting that I am living with you guys when I am not even living in the United States of America, let alone with you guys. Do you both even have the slightest idea of how I have been living in CANADA (Montreal) ever since I got here in September 1995? None. Not that I would have cared or wanted you to do this or that for me. I am not the type; and you should have known better if you cared as much as you are attempting to present to people back home. What is all that for, may I ask?

I have never even been keen on living with people in the first place. I have never even flirted with the idea of coming to live with you guys, if ever [I] decide one day (which is very very unlikely) to permanently move to the United States of America. So, when you guys were even talking on the phone about my saving rents, I was very amused and kept saying to myself: These my people must really be naïve. Only naïve people, I think, would always think that everyone's ambition must coincide with theirs. It might actually be most people's ambition to become American citizens. That is clearly not mine. That may only be a stepping stone to mine, which can be realized without it. What else but naiveté can explain the fact that most people who have not even met me in person now appear to have an idea of what I intend to do with my life; but people like you who are supposedly very close (if I have been living with you since I left Cameroon in 1995, you must be really close indeed) have not the slightest idea or clue? You had better wake up! If you do, you will then be able to realize that you have chosen the wrong person for the acquisition of your cheap popularity.

I just wanted to tell you that you have to wait until I am living with you BEFORE you start using that to get your cheap popularity. NOT BEFORE I am even in the U.S.A., let alone under your roof. I am really annoyed by these wild stories of yours. Are they founded or not?

Sincerely, P.A. FOSSUNGU

P/S: Marie-Claire, on second thought, I think I should send Papa and Schola a copy of this note.

Police-Inspectorizing the Police-Family Theory

Yes, you easily grasp what Petit-Pays' Police-Family Thesis is all about if you properly understand the *giver-receiver* equation between Momany and his sister before the latter ever got to the United States (see Fossungu, 2013c). But Marie-Claire is obviously not alone in the Police-Family business. You have sufficiently also read Scholastica's version, particularly in a previous chapter's *eugenizationing* monologue, which further confirms the artist. You have also heard her conniving in the last chapter to keep Police Inspector Akendung in the dark regarding her coming to America. On his part, this inspector is the best person to understand all the troubles Momany has been through to get this woman through life; but just listen to his own version of the *real* police police-family thesis. Elias Akendung would completely forget that we are family now that I am not a professional like Scholastica with whom he begins dealing financially and otherwise: despite his sound knowledge of the situation the woman has put me (and many others in the family) into. But, like those who create dictators (see Fossungu, 2014b: 126), the policeman does not look far ahead down the road.

On Saturday, November 17, 2012 4:51:50 PM I was surprised to find an email from Julius Ajamah Forbah titled "My second letter from Akendung Elias" in my inbox. It was in all capitals and read:

Hi Peter, Best greetings to you and your family. I hope you are doing well with your wife and children.

Ndi Nkemtaleh Peter, I sent a letter to you on the 8th October 2012 and I am very sure you saw it. Please just tell me if there is any problem between us. I am asking this because I don't know. It's quite a long time you have not called and now that I have written, you can't even reply. I really doubt what is going on. I say again I am very sure you saw the letter I sent on the 8th October 2012 through your e-mail address.

In the letter, I was trying to explain to you the way I am suffering and begging you to help me. I went on retirement since January 2010 and have been in difficulties since then.

Margaret's shop got burnt in the Douala Central Market in the month of June 2011 with goods worth over 3 million. Two months after, the vehicle I was managing with also got burnt. The money I borrowed from meeting houses, that is 2.5 million francs, is yet to be reimbursed. I used the vehicle just for two months before it happened.

My last daughter Mireille is in mission school in form five. The school fees of 420.000 frs is not yet paid and they have already started registering the G.C.E. Ordinary Level. At the opening, I went and begged the principal to allow her in class. The elder sister Doris passed the G.C.E Advanced Level and is doing accountancy in the

University of Buea where I have to pay school fees and house rents.

Thierry is in IRIC Yaoundé. I have to pay his house rents, school fees and feeding. With all these problems, please Peter, I beg you in God's name to try by all means and help me. What are friends and brothers for? Why should I not cry to you when I am in difficulties? I am really suffering, please help me. You can even ask from the Fon of Fossungu. Here is my telephone number: XXXX-XXXX. You know Margaret is a diabetic and high blood patient leaving on drugs always. Please help me I am in fire.

Bye

Hmm! Just hear who is asking: What are friends and brothers for? Why should I not cry to you when I am in difficulties? How schemers forget so easily the harm they do to others. How you become a brother only when it entails their suckering you! 2007 opened my eyes to the way I have to deal with some of these people that hover around you just because they are profiting right away or foresee doing so in the nearest future. I almost got killed in Bonaberi in late January 2007 simply because the police inspector (who had waited alone at the airport for me, drove all the way to the village with me early morning the next day and then quickly returned to Douala without me) was just too tired to come and pick me up in Banaberi on my return to Douala from the village. What are friends and brothers for? But that is not even all of it. I was just lucky to have escaped death and don't exactly know how I was able to reschedule my return to Canada as every dime had been taken away by the thieves. It was not any of the inspector's damn business. But the good tidings would relate to the fact that I was still alive. A former Manjo student hopped out of a taxi in Village (Douala) as I was trekking to nowhere under hot sun. Elizabeth eventually aided me with a sizeable loan the next day that permitted my rearranging my return for the following Wednesday with Swissair in Bonanjo, Douala.

The Wednesday return date came and the inspector accompanied me to the airport. As I approached the control post to get into the area from where boarding takes place, the two police inspectors' question was: "Where is your Canadian Passport?" You would not comprehend my surprise until you know that I did not enter Cameroon as a Canadian. I was in the country as a Cameroonian, using my valid Cameroonian passport. So, where did these police inspectors come about with the idea of my even having a Canadian passport? Of course, the message came home clean and clear when my brother-inspector who has never ever addressed me with any of my numerous titles (as he now does in the email-letter above) quickly cut in with: "Pi, better settle these people before this matter gets too far." It was then I began swiftly connecting the dots and seeing that those in the quarter who had been suggesting that the man surely had a hand in the attack by the thieves might not be totally wrong after all.

Anyway, I was not going to let all that cloud my mind and cause me to play myself into their hands. I fought these police scammers at the airport up to the level of their *commissaire*. I asked them if they are now the Canadian Passport issuing authorities to know that they had issued one of their passports to me. The police commissioner took me to the airline counter where my boarding pass had been issued and was claiming that my Canadian card that I had used as proof that I was entitled to enter Canada had expired. Only some bystanders gave him the mocking of his life with: "*Monsieur le Commissaire, ce document-là ne périme jamais!*" The police commissioner became so ashamed of himself that he actually escorted me like they do to a Minister to the waiting area, past the trio of inspectors that were taken aback as I royally found myself on the other side of their heavily guarded passage back to Canada: "without settling them" whatsoever.

That is how the above-mentioned no-communication was initialized; how the 2014 trips got a different type of announcement and welcome; and perhaps how before I reached Canada in 2007 another court battle had already been scheduled by the London woman called Scholastica because "He went to Cameroon with a lot of money that he was attacked by thieves." From whom do you think Scholastica got the vibes? But that is not the reason I did not respond to the inspector's first email-letter; a missive which I had not seen because of reasons made known in my response to the one you have just read. On Thursday, January 10, 2013 at 1.06 AM I wrote in "Re: My Second Letter from Akendung Elias", stating:

Hi Inspector Elias:

Sorry I am seeing your email only now. My inbox is completely flooded with emails from last two years because I scarcely get into it every day. Sorry also for all the mishaps. Above all, sorry that I am not in any position to help. As you may well know, the woman I brought to this country got here and decided that I will spend all my life working just for her and her parents, brothers and sisters. Remember too she used to take money from you but when she got here she behaved as if the debt with you (as well others contracted here in Canada, and another there in Cameroon through her friend, Edith Khumbah for her trip) had absolutely nothing to do

127

with her. I know Scholastica and her parents have made it a point to paint me as the worst person on earth; and if others buy their lies, that is not a problem because they may not have the facts. But you, at least, have the raw facts.

I would really like to aid but I cannot; maybe she can.

Nkemtale'eh.

If the inspector's conscience was not really eating him up like hungry lions devour a captured prey, what was the commotion he created when I reached Douala in May 2014 at Nkemanang's residence all about? He came there one early morning (after having surprisingly met me on the street) and threatened to burn the man's house if I (who was then in there still sleeping because of the time difference) do not settle him completely for the millions he claimed I was still owing to him in regard of my wife, Scholastica! How this love for money can reduce some people to zero! Did he forget too that I had paid his money through Western Union and still had all the papers available? That he was the one who had been telling people left and right how I had paid the entire sum *without adding a franc in excess*? Even under-twelve-year children in that compound all made fun of this retired policeman, saying "*Na just becos Papa Peter don come stay na for we house weh di make dis man craze-soh?*" We would certainly not talk about anything else if I want to exhaust the *Akendunging* police-family tale of Cameroon's Turbo d'Afrique, as Petit-Pays also calls himself.

But Petit-Pays is certainly not the lone advocate though. Germaine La Belle calls herself 'Men's Advocate'. Singing in her electrifying and very danceable *Les Hommes*, Germaine La Belle calls on her fellow women to respect their husbands by giving them their rightful place in the union since God intended different roles for the sexes. The Vatican, for example, would all along be seeming to agree with La Belle until the Holy See would be engulfed in a maelstrom of scandals in early 2013 in which the pope's personal butler leaked a huge cache of embarrassing documents to the Italian press, and a 300-page report exposed a "'gay network' of ranking clerics" that indulges in "regular sex parties" and exerts "'undue influence' in the Curia", leading to Benedict becoming the first pope in nearly 600 years to resign (Linker, 2015).

From Step-Mother to Wife and from Woman to Man: What Shall I Call Them?

The list of the singers is lengthy. But let's close it with Prince Aimé who calls himself the People's Counsellor. In *La Polygamie* he sings about the dangerous consequences of having more than one wife, and some Nigerian filmmakers have variously depicted the problems too in several films, including *The Pains of Polygamy*. In short, the whole issue graphically turns on the struggle (declared or undeclared) between African and externally imposed cultural norms. According to C.S. Lewis, "There ought to be two distinct kinds of marriage: one governed by the State with rules enforced by all citizens, the other governed by the Church with rules enforced by her on her own members" (cited in Westbrook, 2010: 2). Cameroon would go further and say three types as you hear from a love and marriage specialist. *Chantomapheticism* was simply killing Momany so softly that he just "wanted to meet her [Chantal's] parents in order to traditionally (if not officially) bring her home" (Fossungu, 2014: 114). Three types of marriages are recognized in

Cameroon: customary, religious, and official. It is one's choice to go through any or all of them but, usually, most people only proceed with the others in church/mosque and in the mayor's office (often combined) after the customary rites have been fulfilled. That explains why Momany wanted to meet Chantal's parents 'in order to traditionally (if not officially) bring her home' (Fossungu, 2014: 114).

In 1998 a critic of Africa's claim to *trijuralism* made some telling assertions that would greatly aid us in understanding the cultural issues here. By *trijuralism*, one would be describing a situation where three different law regimes or systems co-exist in the same socio-political field (that is, a country). And for Cameroon, the claim is that there are (1) *Droit Coutumier*, (2) *Droit Civil*, and (3) Common Law (Fossungu, 1998). African cultural norms would be embodied in what is generally known here as *droit coutumier* that would be said to be in competition with official or state law (common law & civil law, for Cameroon, as it is claimed). The question firmly posed earlier relates to whether courts are equipped with the necessary skills and other attributes to be able to also resolve disputes between these groups on the African side of the wide Atlantic. The issue, to reiterate, revolves between those who favour cultural traditionalism and those who prefer modernity (or foreign cultures), with the courts, of course, playing no role worth examining, as Ewang, Bongyu and Buhnyuy would tell us.[40]

The matter is even easily cleared off the table with what one expert called "Confused Cameroon Law" in a 1998 piece

---

[40] See Andrew Sone Ewang, Godwin Moye Bongyu and Juliette Suliy Buhnyuy, "The Judiciary as the Last Hope for the Protection of Democracy and Human Rights in Cameroon" 3(1) *Cameroon Journal on Democracy and Human Rights* (2009), 36-46.

in *The Herald* in which he argued at length against the claim that *trijuralism* exists in Cameroon:

> Well, I don't know how correct that claim [of *trijuralism* and of the courts upholding it] is, but I think I have a small story that can help us [to] find out. There is the case of this [University of Yaoundé] law graduate whom villagers would consider (and rightly so) as an educated illiterate. He happens to be in the village when a land dispute arises. The village council and chief settle the case as is usual for them to do.
>
> But the law graduate gets up (full of his empty University of Yaounde Law) and challenges the decision on the basis that, as none of the two disputants could produce a land title (*titre foncier* as he would prefer to say in order to bamboozle those unschooled villagers), the said land becomes village property. Perfectly the right thing in the wrong place. Hardly is customary law as such taught in the country's law faculties. There is then tension between these "customary lawyers" and the customary-law illiterate "modern lawyers".
>
> The examples could be endless; and there would be no need trying to multiply them here. But the question is: just how is this *trijuralism* operating here? I should like to take the time to draw your attention to the fact that this is the same person who will tomorrow be sitting on our bench and applying the only law he knows to all the cases: after having bribed his way into and through ENAM [the National School of Administration and Magistracy]. Such schizophrenic drive to apply only the "judge's law" to all situations would also help in its own way to divide rather

than integrate Cameroonians. *Trijuralism* indeed! Would *bijuralism* also stand? (Fossungu, 1998: 4)

If apparent *bijuralism* is now something the authorities just can't live with,[41] what is to be made of/about *quadrijuralism*? By this, I mean the logical addition of C.S. Lewis' marriage 'governed by the Church with rules enforced by her on her own members' to *trijuralism*. In addition to its proscription of polygamy, the religious teachings of the Church also have it, for example, that a brother cannot have anything sexual with his brother's wife, let alone taking her for a wife. Thus, Washington's Cardinal Wuerl in March 2015 told us that "Saint John the Baptist reminded King Herod that he could not just take his brother's wife. The woman and the king had John put to death" (Wuerl, 2015). This wife-taking issue is particularly one where the African side of the marriage and family narrative is hinged, resulting from some aspects of ACM (African Customary Marriage), epitomized by polygamy. When American singer, Dionne Warwick, sang her *Shall I Tell?* (which I would rather modify to "What shall I call Them?"), I think she must have had African (and more precisely Bangwa royal) tradition and Same-Sex Marriage (SSM) families in mind. I will eschew being corrupted by *culturignorantism*, the well-known disease associated to "presidentially appointed so-called cultural advisers (who will

---

[41] In an article in the *Cameroon Journal*, Sylvanus Ezieh on February 27, 2015 wrote that "The Common Law practice in Cameroon has again suffered a major setback. After Common Law Lawyers protested an attempt by the Biya's regime to impose notaries on the English Legal System last year, Anglophone Lawyers in the North West Region are now being compelled to make their court submissions only in the French language." http://www.cameroonjournal.com/exclusive-english-language-banned-in-nw-courts-lawyers-to-make-submissions-in-french-only/. See also Fossungu (2013a: chapter 4).

usually know nothing even about the culture of the specific ethnic groups they come from, let alone those of the entire country)" (Fossungu, 2013a: 13), by mostly limiting myself to the cultural practices I know well – my own *Bangwa Kinship and Marriage*, to adopt Robert Brian's 1972 book's title.

Nowadays, young children are finding it really hard to know exactly what to call other siblings or others in the household: Is it sister/brother, cousin, or cousin-sister/brother, (mother or father, in the case of American SSM[42]). This is the result of some *questionable* aspects of tradition (succession and inheritance) that, I think, are happily being sent to the dustbin – thanks very much to Fon Nicasius Nguazong Fossungu of Nwangong who assumed the throne in 2008. But the never-going-away question still lingers on. Would the new, young and educated Fon *alone* suffice to obliterate this centuries-old tradition? This question is very important to address since, as Donald Cardinal Wuerl has very eloquently put it in the SSM arena, "This is not new teaching – but it is challenging. Human sexuality is a gift and every generation finds the desire for sexual activity to be strong and inviting. For some, it can be even overpowering. Often the teachings of the Church flowing from the words of her Lord strike some as confining, even distasteful. So it has always been" (Wuerl, 2015). Yes. The Archbishop of Washington makes the point so well if you remember always that a king or chief or fon never dies in Africa. He simply

---

[42] "Some heterosexuals just don't know what world they are in, hearing two hefty men there, one calling the other my *wife*! And a woman like Rosie O being called 'my husband' by another woman. Wife and husband indeed" (Fossungu, 2015a: 131; emphasis is original). Now, how easy do you expect a child (originally from a heterosexual home but who is now adopted by the homosexuals) to naturally/normally call Rosie O 'father', or one of the hefty men 'mother'?

goes on a journey and comes back younger than he went, it is there said. Could this be the main reason why his *replacement* has to continue with everything of his, including taking on his wives? From step-mother to wife!

It is essential to register also that the one who succeeds a Fon 'who has travelled' is just one of his numerous sons (and daughters). And that – in heavy contrast to King Herod – if the new Bangwa Fon refuses (like Fon NN Fossungu has) to *formally* inherit the women of his predecessor, there are two things that often happen to produce the same head-scattering results or consequences. Either (1) his other brothers (as well as other close relations such as cousins and uncles) quickly jump on these women and/or (2) the women themselves scramble for his brothers and the others. Welcome then to Nwangong Fondom for some *oddifacism* of marriage and family that would move in parallel to those of SSM over which the courts in America have been called to preside.

The Bangwa are in Debundschazone of Cameroon. Fossungu (2013b) has lengthily described their federalist tradition which would also mainly explain their numerous palaces. In that book also the author quotes Robert Brian who theorizes that "A Bangwa claims no clan or lineage membership, and no corporate group takes responsibility for any of his or her actions. Kinship is an aid to the business of making a living: trading, inheriting, acquiring a title, farming, ruling and marrying. And as the business of living is complex in Bangwa so is the kinship system" (Fossungu, 2013b: 122 n.134). Without independent courts or other similar institutions (as is often presented in western narratives), one would begin to wonder how people function and survive in a complex system as the Bangwa's here. But the matter is very simple if we put ignorance and bigotry aside and attempt to understand how things work in environments dissimilar to ours. The counsel here ties in with Cardinal Wuerl's concern with recent trends in America. According to the Washington Man of God, "today there is a new challenge. Some who reject the Church's teaching – who choose to live by another set of values – not only find the voice of Christian values annoying, they would like to see it silenced or at least muted. Thus we have a whole new upside down version of words like 'discrimination,' 'freedom' and 'human rights,' and laws to enforce the new meaning" (Wuerl, 2015).

That is the exact same thing Africans suffered in the hands of the same Church that was aiding colonisation and calling the African way of life barbaric, needing to be civilized (destroyed, that is). Those Africans that resisted this process were branded as barbarians and murderers. I use the past tense not because it is all over. Noam Chomsky can take over here and tell you more about its persistence as it also relates to NNA and its Aboriginals and Blacks: while I focus on Africa's Bangwa. My uncle, Nkemanang, who resides in Douala, is a notable in the Fondom of Nwangong. Precisely, he is an *nkem*; thus he is known as Nkemanang. Apart from another *nkem* residing also in Douala called Nkemazigou Thomas Ekwe, I do not know of another personality that takes tradition more seriously than Nkemanang. You already know that in July 2014 I was in Cameroon for the funeral ceremony of my biological mother. During the multi-sectional event, I discovered many *surprising* things within my royal family. One of these relates to my uncle's sibling that would be hard to classify within the western definition of sibling. When my grandfather, Fon ST Fossungu, passed away in 1979, his successor (Fon DF Fossungu who is Nkemanag's brother) took Nkemanang's mother (as the other widows) for a wife and had Child A (a girl) with her. So Child A is my aunty and cousin? She is also Nkemanag's half-sister and half-cousin? Nkemanang is my uncle because he is my grandfather's son and my dad's brother.

But the categorization complication does not seem to end there. On Fon DF Fossungu's death in 2007, one of his sons (my cousin) now called Fonkwetta had a real duel with Nkemanang over the youngest of the late Fon's wives (call her Wife X). Fonkwetta who is based in the village got the upper hand and is already having children with Wife X, one of whom is a girl called Child B. Taking the present scenario before the imagined one later, what is Fonkwetta's actual relationship with his own daughter from Wife X (Fonkwetta's step-mother-turned-wife)? In other words, is Child B a daughter to Fonkwetta as well as his half-sister? Are Children A and B cousins, aunt-niece, or what? Assuming now that it is Nkemanang who got Wife X and had Child C (a boy) with her, what is the relationship of Child C to Child A? You can continue to multiply the family relationship *oddifacism* while I aid your comprehension through briefly describing the umbrella captions.

The CGAM Debt Recovery Fiasco and the Catch-All African Umbrella

I am here calling Nkemanang my uncle but he always refers to me as "brother". This is understandable for a number of reasons. The first is that he is the age-mate of my direct follower from the same biological mother. Again, in Africa generally, most relationships are buried under "brother" and "sister" (this connotation does not quite encapsulate the exploitative use of these terms, as I have more elaborately discussed in chapter 2 of *The HISOFE Dictionary of Midnight Politics*), and "parent" and "child". Very few people in the village especially go the extra mile to specifically distinguish these relationships, most probably because there a child is not just that of the parents that combined in the 'doing of bad thing' to bring him/her into the world. It is the child of the community.

Therefore, any elder who finds a child misbehaving takes it as his/her responsibility to correct (or discipline) the child without the biological parents making a fuss of the situation. It is probably because of this worldview (and to also stem promiscuity of family members) that some of the awkward relationships (in Western eyes) noted here do not appear as such to those concerned. But no culture is static, and the younger generation (greatly exposed to other 'patronizing' cultures as we all know) is posing stiff questions that have to and must be answered. It is perhaps through important exercises such this present endeavour that some of those people who are consciously or inadvertently creating some of these hard-to-classify family relations could realize what they are doing. This is an enterprise that could not have been possible without the unique voyage of discovery that engendered the need to study ACM alongside NNA's SSM that is now one of the most litigated issues. We will be coming back to this litigation in the next chapter after finishing business with the finances of CGAM and the operation of birth-marriage *sociopackism*.

Membership Termination by Expulsion: The Kangong, Najeme et al., and Others Affairs

To better understand the debt recovery question, you need to be familiar with expulsion politics in the CGAM since the two (at least, in the case of the *Najeme et al Affair*) are linked up. To the minds of all post-2005 admitted members, the word expulsion would quickly bring the 2007-2008 transition wrangling that is known as *The Najeme et al Affair*. But I must inform these members that some of the 2007 bureau members involved would not be the first opportunity that has been presented to the GGA of the CGAM to expel an unbecoming member. I would guess that these ineffective and woeful 2008 cases (implicit in the *Anung resignaspension* below) were clearly drawing from the failure of the initial or original case (*Kangong-Wilfred Affair*) which was all due to members not being able to apply the law without fear or favour.

The Kangong-Wilfred Affair had to do with Wilfred Kangong's insulting and menacing comportment to the House generally but especially towards the president, who had simply questioned his gross failure to play host to the Assembly as expected. At the March 2005 GGA, a committee that had been appointed to look into the hosting issue between CGAM (represented by the president – Paul Takha Ayah) and Wilfred Kangong, presented its report that was normally to be followed by a decision to expel or not. Valentine Usongo was head of that committee and presented its recommendations as follows (GGA Minutes):

-   That no direct accusations were made to Kangong Wilfred as stipulated in his e-mail

- That the committee was embarrassed by the threats from Wilfred
- That the committee was very disgruntled with the situation
- That Kangong Wilfred should withdraw his e-mails, statements of threat and should apologize to goodwill for his acts.

The reactions from the report, according to the Minutes, were heated with a "serious debate on this issue" and the following points were retained:

- Denis Alem suggested committee should meet and take action about previous exchanges because they failed to look into details; this assertion was supported by Fidelis Folifac.

- Vincent [Cheg Ncheg] suggested findings of committee were ok and that Wilfred should apologize

- Hans [Najeme] addressed [the GGA and] spoke about the exchanges and requested that the topic should be closed

- Peter Fossungu emphasized they dealt with issue [of expulsion] as requested.

- The president intervened and suggested a vote be conducted on the basis that the findings of the committee be accepted or rejected.

The vote was 15 members against versus 5 for the findings.

- Wilfred kangong [then] took the floor, explained he could not host because he just had a baby and showed a mail supporting his claim. Ayuk Ako-Arrey suggested he should not be blamed if there was such a mail circulated.

Atemba Patricia suggested such exchanges should never happen again through e-mails.

- Jackson Atam suggested president should not have dropped the phone on Wilfred and should apologize on behalf of goodwill for that, meanwhile another committee should meet again to take decisions.

After deliberations a vote was conducted on whether both parties should apologize to each other or Wilfred should be the one to apologize to goodwill.

The result of the vote was 12 for both parties to apologize versus 5 for Wilfred only.

Both parties tendered their apologies and also extended a hand shake and the matter was closed.

The Najeme-Hans et al Palaver: Clearly, in my view, the Assembly lost an invaluable opportunity to set the rules straight in the *Kangong Affair*, sending a dangerous message that would explain why no one has been expelled without people seeing it as settlement of personal scores, as was particularly evoked in the *Najeme et al* palaver. The Najeme *et al* case would fit the said description because everything done was viewed more or less in the nature of "settlement of personal scores" using CGAM: see the various write-ups provoked by President Folefac's communication titled '*2007 audit updates*' that hit the airwave on November 23, 2008.[43] I

---

[43] On November 27, 2008 a former president wrote on the issue:
Hi everyone,

It is unfortunate that this issue has degenerated into name-calling with a lot of emotions. I think a number of clarifications will help to shed light on things and put an end to the name-calling. 1. During the first audit I conducted, I called Karen [Najeme] and verified the cheque in question and I was satisfied that it was repaid based on all the details she provided. 2. During the second audit that I did together with Chris

would not even want to venture near the drama/counter-drama in an earlier GGA that "expelled" said individuals "in absentia", *motionly*, of course. Did they realize that no such expulsion was foreseen by the CGAM constitution? Wasn't this just copycatting the Biya farce in Cameroon with Ahidjo's condemnation and sentence in absentia for 'plotting against the security of the state'? The *Kangong Affair* clearly answers the constitutional question in the negative. Wilfred was right there when the expulsion decision was being made and the decision was reached through voting, not a 'seconded motion'. The manner in which some of these things occurred would make it very hard not to believe the personal-scores-settlement theorists; the more so when you consider Fidelis Folefac's comportment in the *Tanyi-Patrick Affair*, an expulsion case that is popularly known as *In the Matter of Children's Christmas Party*:

Concerning the incident that happened at the Children's end of year party, members of the general assembly expressed their disapproval for the act and

---

[Ntohgno] and Margaret [Egbe Enow?], no such verification was done. 3. Given that both audits are being contested, I feel it was only normal for any issues of concern to be re-submitted to the external auditor. 4. Regarding the cancellation of the May 2007 meeting, all the evidence confirms the fact that the meeting was cancelled in early May (after the cheque had already been issued) and not during the April meeting. 5. I feel that as Goodwill president, Fidelis is acting in the best int[er]est of Goodwill and his action should not be construed as a personal vendetta. 6. Given the time lapse since May last year, it is only normal that memories are not quite fresh about what may have transpired before the May 2007 meeting was called off. I hope this clarification helps to cool emotions and I call on those concerned to show restraint.

Regards,
Paul Ayah

called on the constitutional Article that addresses matters of this nature [to] be appl[ied].

The meeting went in complete chaos, when Mr Patrick Tanyi emotionally burst into tears while explaining his own version of the story.

Mr. Fidelis Folifac called on a motion that the general assembly has inappropriately called "his brother" to testify in the public [and] he said it was humiliating, incorrect and unacceptable. He walked out of the General assembly in disapproval.

The President tabled the issue for a vote at the general assembly. A vote was conduct and the majority voted for the expulsion of Mr. Patrick Tanyi (GGA Minutes January 2011).

From the foregoing, it is worthless talking further about the *Najeme case*, except to show the laughing-stocking nature of rule enforcement in the CGAM – a sort of good preparation for you to successfully jump upon/into the CGAM Night Flight/Train to Visionless Land called *Constitutionadhocism* and *Postponemetolodrama*. A lot of people in CGAM and the larger African community in Montreal pretend not to understand the Najeme Bureau Affair. I am here talking about the *midnighters*. Those who sometimes claim to understand it just do not know what they are talking about. I am here referring to the simpletons who follow without knowing where they are being led to. Since this bureau has already been largely analyzed (see Fossungu, 2015: chapters 3 & 4), I will limit myself here to just showing that these embezzlers knew very well that those who were trying to recover debts or embezzled funds from them just could not. Would *tree-toppers* not know themselves so well? Just listen to the pretenders in the July 2008 GGA in Gatineau to realize what I am leading you into. The Gatineau minutes were prepared by Florence Nakam and would tell us about internal debt recovery. We are in Canada my friends, and the CGAM is not operating illicitly and the courts of this country are there to take care of situations like this one, I inform them. They then tell you that "We don't want to drag our brother(s) to court." So what are they really after then? Midnight business settlement, isn't it?

Over to Gatineau 2008 where you will learn that President Folefac said the executive committee is doing their best to recover money and stay civilly responsible; that the president, vice president and one of the internal auditors received a letter from Mr Hans Najeme's lawyer contesting the findings of the audit. The president also said they were invited to mediation by ACC Permanent Council which is ongoing. He briefed GGA members that the past president (Najeme) has contested the basis of the audit, with argument that his executive had not submitted their final financial statement [GGA Minutes]. Did you just hear them? They are brotherly avoiding the courts when their "brother" already has a lawyer between himself and them. Bullshit also to even be involving the Association of Cameroonians in Canada (ACC) which everyone knows has this notorious record of *politickerizing* with everything. That is precisely why *they* call some of us hardliners. When you must have read: *The HISOFE Dictionary of Midnight Politics*, then you would better understand what I am saying, since we would not even be at this point but for their endless propensity to *politickerize*.

Otherwise, why is the Najeme debt issue so pushed to the front when this is not the only debt to be recovered by the same Folefac administration? Hear the July 2009 Assembly deliberations:

The Fin[ancial] department notified the GGA of some members who do not comply... [with] loan reimbursement. Several attempts for these members to refund the loan have failed. The first was that of Mrs Nkoh Angeline who issued a bounce[d] check. Ma Angel explained to GGA that she lost her job because of her health situation and was unable to pay the loan in time. She further expressed her readiness to pay the loan and pleaded to the GGA to give her a month since she just picked up a new job. The GGA accepted her request and gave her one month to pay the loan (GGA Minutes July 2009).

But this same loan will be reaching the next administration in 2010 when the debtor would not only have been admitted as a member (contrary to regulations) but it would also require the creation of a *third* Loan Recovery Committee, chaired by Enongene Ekwe, to seek to collect the said money (see GGA Minutes April 2010). Are you then wondering what the Gatineau Assembly has to do under this head? The Gatineau agenda also highlighted the expulsion of the secretary general from the bureau and that is principally why we were there. But I think these guys had already been *controversially* expelled in absentia in an earlier Assembly? Good question. As stated in Fossungu (2015b), when you govern an association or any other body with its constitution, you clearly do not need to rigmarole to make your points. Otherwise, inconsistencies would be written all over the place. Thus, the president would be there in Gatineau instead explaining that the mediators were informed that a financial statement had been submitted and emailed to all members by the past Financial Secretary. But, to continue to show the good faith of Goodwill in the recovery process, the president said the former president was given up to June 30, starting from June 14, to submit a new financial statement, else the independent external audit will be based on what had been circulated to all members. The president read out the draft protocol to the assembly and said they were yet to agree on who will pay the initial audit fee. Following the terms of the draft, he suggested that it will be nice for Goodwill to pay so as not to give any room for further delays. The assembly gave a vote of confidence to the executive to keep up with the recovery process, ensure that the mediation process is efficient else proceed to small claims court. The motion of support to the executive action came from Johnson Ngalla seconded by Jules Komguep (Gatineau Minutes).

The *Anung Resignaspension* and the Family-Neglect Theory

And what happened to the expulsion of the S-G from the bureau? Nothing at all, it was rather the famous resignation of S-G Wilson Anung that came to them through electronic mail. I can see that you are set for the judging. Please, kindly therefore step into the *Resignaspension* Bus that is here to better school you in the Politics of Family Neglect, and more. This *resignaspension* (or whatever you want to call it) would help your understanding of certain dynamics and fallouts (1) of the first ever hotly contested elections in CGAM, (2) of the first ever president booted out of office after just one term, (3) of what democracy means to CGAMers, and (4) of out-of-CGAM-meeting meetings that seek to *Ahidjolistically* impinge on the management and direction of the CGAM. Most of these issues will come out from both the accusations and the president's response to them. Let's first get what the chief executive would be responding to by letting Anung himself to articulate things to you (the jumping in numbering is original):

Fellow Members of Goodwill,

Good day to everybody! Today Saturday the 21st day of the month of June 2008, I, Mr. Wilson Anung ha[ve] decided to step down from the post of the secretary general of Cameroon Goodwill Association of Montreal. Some of the major reasons for my resignation are as follows:

1. The financial saga that is prevailing in Goodwill: Wilson Anung is not ready to be a member of a team whose main priority is to sabotage and defame people's reputation. I believe [that] in Goodwill if the General Assembly mandates the executive, for any major decision, this has to be done through a vote as prescribed by the constitution. It has been a habit of this executive to claim that the General Assembly mandates them for decisions they have been taking. We all know that this so-called mandate is always done by motion[] which doesn't reflect the general will of the assembly. In a true democracy, motions are meant to be debated and voted upon for them to be binding. I for one will not stand by and see the executive disregard the constitution and only apply certain parts they perceive will suit their objectives or personal interests. This association was created as a family meeting for Cameroonians to come together once in a month and socialize. By dismissing members who

have worked very hard for the association and at the same time threatening to drag them to court is a move that will never be supported by Wilson Anung, hence he cannot be part of such a team.

3. It is clear that some people want to use Goodwill as a tool to settle personal scores. Wilson Anung is not prepared to be used by somebody or a group of individuals as a weapon to fight personal differences.

4. My family was completely ignored during the Mother's Day celebration. How can someone understand the fact that during the aforementioned celebration there was a "Fashion Parade" that was organized and we have two daughters at home who could have fully participated in the show but no one contacted me or my wife to ask about their availability? That means, my family is not recognized as Goodwillers so why should I be rendering services to an association that does not recognize my family? My wife's name appeared in the first list that came out for women who were to cook for the occasion and when a second list was out, her name was, by design, scraped off. That means my family is being marginalized, so why should I work for the association?

5. I have come to realize that I am being marginalized by the current executive board even though people try to pretend to be working hand-in-gloves with me. That explains why I see no reason to be part of such a team.

6. The president has a tendency of calling executive meetings frequently and during week days, knowing full[] well that I have a tight schedule during the week. This puts me in a unique position to step down as the secretary general because I have a job and a family responsibility. I am not an idle person and Goodwill is not my career. The

list is inexhaustible. I have decided not to bore members with excessive reading. The bottom line is that I have resigned as the secretary general of Goodwill. Information reaching me from various sources say[s] that people are planning to move a motion for Wilson Anung to be fired from the post of the secretary general. In a clear note I will like to remind members of Goodwill that I did not come into office by a motion that was moved. I was democratically elected in an election that was highly contested, the first of its kind that has gone into the history of Goodwill. That said, if members of Goodwill feel that I am not doing my job properly then I will need the 41 electorates to cast me a vote of no confidence because before my accession to power, out of the 80 electorates that participated in the election I secured 41 votes and the runner-up had 39.

I have just one apology to make. This apology goes to those who gave me the mandate to pilot the affairs of this association as a secretary general. I fully understand the depth of the damage this resignation is going to cause in your hearts. Please accept my apology. We are still together in other capacities, particularly, as fellow brothers and sisters of Cameroon origin.

N/B: With immediate effect I am also suspending my Goodwill membership indefinitely.

Done today Saturday June 21, 2008 in LaSalle, Montreal.

Signature

Wilson Anung

A hard copy will be sent in as soon as possible.

That was the entire *resignaspension*. Whoever said CGAMers did not know their rights and obligations? Whatever other questions you are already posing in your mind must wait till after President Folefac's response that attempted to tackle the claims. The introductory part of this response dealing with the indefinite membership suspension can be found in Fossungu (2015a: 119-120). The rest is as follows:

Financial saga, personal differences and decision-making in the general assembly

Please members refer to the minutes of the March, 2008 meeting prepared by Mr. Anung that gave the executive the mandate to recover the money. It is very unfortunate that we are witnessing these distortions. Suffice to mention that we need not remind anyone of privileged information that has been made public regarding Goodwill funds and compensation.

We will like to assure Goodwillers that although some members of the executive have been particularly labelled and threatened on the recovery of the unaccounted amount, we will stay focus[ed], and ensure that the process is fairly executed. No amount of name calling, distortions and threats will make us fold and no one shall be allowed to use the name of Goodwill to fake, fight or solve what has been termed personal differences.

To show our diligence and fairness, we have accepted a request from and are taking part in mediation by the ACC Permanent Council. Together with the former president we are close to completing a protocol that may lead to a new audit of the 2007 finances by an accredited independent firm. All parties have also agreed that the same firm will independently audit all 2007 fund-raising Ad-hoc committees.

On the issue of decision-making, it is the right of every member to express their opinion on ALL topics discussed in the assembly, if a member fails to object on the floor, to enable voting on the matter, Goodwill can, regrettably not be able to sympathize with ideas discussed out of the meeting. As you all know, in the absence of any contrary ideas on an issue, including the adoption of minutes, the issue under review is unanimously adopted by the assembly through a motion that is seconded.

Family not recognised by Goodwill and wife's name 'by design scraped off' May Party cooking list

To claim that he cannot render services to an association that does not recognize his family is surprising because it is only recently that Goodwill issued a social (birth) assistance check of the full amount to his family. Furthermore, his wife's name is on the cooking list for monthly meetings. However, we will look into the allegation that Mrs. Anung's name was, 'by design, scraped off' the cooking list of the May party.

Lastly, there are over 65 children in Goodwill and less than 7 children took part in the parade during the May party. Even at the International Children's Day celebration, it was not possible to have all our children on the stage. So were the rest of the children slighted? We encourage parents to be proactive in updating the list of Goodwill children and to encourage and facilitate their children['s] participation in events because usually parents need to drop off their children for rehearsals.

Integration in the executive and career

First, Mr. Anung had been properly informed, through the minutes of the May 22 executive meeting that during the June general assembly meeting, the executive will present the current state of the SG participation to the assembly.

Some of the concerns being that since he was elected into office, he has only attended (came late) one executive meeting, as such each time someone else had to perform his tasks. We have one executive meeting per month (is this frequent?) and the date of the meeting is chosen by the majority of the executive, not the President. To claim otherwise only shows how he is out of touch with the functioning of the executive. Goodwillers should remember that the Sec. Gen. is custodian of the association's facts and figures and disseminating proper information to its members. He is the channel through which the executive board communicates to the general assembly. If the Sec. Gen. does not attend executive meetings what kind of information will he pass on to its members? In keeping with team spirit principles, from time to time we have been forced to fill the vacuum created by his consistent absence but felt that the GGA should be adequately updated on this during the June meeting.

Also, minutes of previous GGA meetings are hardly sent out one week prior to the next meeting as the constitution demands. Corrected and adopted minutes have never been made available to the webmaster for uploading on the website.

Furthermore, the Exco had to, in January and February general assembly meetings, solicit the services of a non-executive member to take the minutes while waiting for the SG, and in April, we delayed the start of the meeting due to his lateness.

On the issue of career, serving Goodwill has also been on voluntary basis with no incentives, except otherwise. Unlike previous years when people were nominated and sometimes persuaded to serve, this year people willingly applied and made electoral promises. Despite our personal responsibilities, we take the pleasure and commit to effectively serve Goodwillers with determination and our ability to deliver.

Way forward

Because there is currently no provision in the constitution on the procedure of filling a vacant post, we have asked Goodwill Advisory Council to propose a policy for adoption during the July thematic meeting to [e]nable us fill this vacancy.

In conclusion, we appreciate all of you for the relentless effort and support to move this family association to greater heights. Let no one be distracted by any agenda-driven misconception. In unity we will stand and make Goodwill a better association for our families with transparency and accountability being our watchwords.

Thanks and God bless you.

Goodwill Executive [bold and underlining are original].

GACing Birth-Marriage *Sociopackism*: Egyptian-Kingism, Doublesidism or Stark Failure in Duty?

The GAC: If the discussion so far is only disturbing in regard of the *Folefacist* administration, then its handling of the born-house and marriage *sociopackism* doubtlessly is the bureau's waterloo. *GACing* derives from the GAC (Goodwill Advisory Council) and a brief survey of this body would surely facilitate your digestion of the waterloo thesis. Governed by Article 9, GAC is composed of registered founding members in good standing and past presidents of Goodwill in good financial standing. Its functions are many. GAC ensures that the highest ethical standards are maintained by all officials of Goodwill and ensures a smooth transition between the out-going and in-coming Executive Bureau. The chair of GAC rotates and is based on the seniority of founding members and presidential seniority. GAC performs an advisory role to the executive and in conflict resolution. I think the best way to give you a better insight into this organ will be through the entire report of the a very important November 2011 GAC meeting from its out-going chair, Peter A. Fossungu, sent to the other GAC members, with this message: 'Hi everyone, Please, check this document to see if I did not forget anything and then let the current chair follow up from here'.[44] GAC's functions are

---

[44] The said minutes of one of the GAC's Meeting are below:
GAC MEETING
Date: Saturday 5 November 2011
Venue and Time: Bloom Talent's Office from 10.30 am to 3.30 pm
Purpose: Audit (GAC restructure and other means of making the Association more efficient)
The following points were tabled, discussed and recommended:
The Association

153

Goodwill mandate has to change in order to enable the association to still exercise its singular influence, notwithstanding the proliferation of associations in the community. It can do so, for instance, by enabling other "sister" groups benefit from its contacts and other advantages such as the free hall for events from the LaSalle Council. Therefore, presidents of said associations should be invited to a meeting with the Goodwill bureau before submission of its calendar [of] activities requiring the hall (which would have also accommodated said associations' need).

The sound system has to be sold since it is not being used and the association spends money in its storage.

Association's Executive

The size of the bureau should be reduced to five members, namely, president, secretary general, financial secretary, treasurer, and organizing secretary; with a two-year mandate.

The constitutional article on loss of membership consequent on five-consecutive non-payment of dues should be scrupulously applied by the bureau.

The 'political issue' was determined as follows. GAC has to draw its conclusion on it before Saturday GA meeting and discuss with the executive (president) beforehand by email so they could prepare how to answer to it during that GA meeting.

Goodwill FC

The initial suggestion was that its status be reviewed so that its membership should be tied to membership of Goodwill. It was finally resolved that it be left open as is currently the case but that Goodwill need to have its hand firmly on the club through budgetary allocations as well as its patron, president, and manager making their presence felt. As concerns the budget, two hundred and fifty dollars (250.00$) should be made available from Goodwill for sponsoring in-door soccer and five hundred dollars (500.00$) for tournaments that have also to coincide with Goodwill activities such as annual barbecue.

GAC Structure

The sitting president of Goodwill has to be member of GAC

GAC should have quarterly meetings which will be used to conduct internal auditing of the association and will be reported to the GGA.

GAC will have a rotating chair with a one-year term. The chair will be assisted by a rapporteur who immediately becomes the next chair. The current chair is President Edward Takang with Dr. Walter Ndonkeu as rapporteur.

Recognition certificates, though still a matter for the sitting president to decide, will nevertheless be more formal through its being discussed with the GAC.

more understood from the angle of a watch dog over the smooth functioning of the activities of the organization. Its meetings are exclusive to non-members except in one area (handing over ceremony) where all CGAMers and even non-CGAMers are invited to participate. Now, let us get back to *sociopackism*.

Born-House in the General Assembly: During the January 2006 GGA, *Born House* (as birth *sociopackism* is popularly called) was top on the discussions. I must again point out that this meeting was important for being one at which the GGA was debating and adopting recommendations put before it by the first BRC (Bylaws Revision Committee) chaired by Hans Najeme (with the Ndonkeu-Folefac connexion). Until then most constitutional revisions were usually proposed or introduced by the Executive Bureau through inclusion in the agenda and discussed and adopted or rejected in the GGA. This January Assembly was thus not only positively innovative but also negatively somewhat officialising the *blackletterism* that I have protractedly mentioned elsewhere (see Fossungu, 2015b).

Structural changes that are constitutional in nature would have to be incorporated during the next review of the constitution but those that are just matters of internal administration would be incorporated right away into the association's by-laws.

President Folefac opted to commence with the financial audit while Dr. Ndonkeu handles property audit.

General

The very fruitful meeting had the unique entertaining of Mr. Roger Ngwesse (current financial secretary and the only invited bureau member who could physically make it) who also contributed ideas in no small way. President Florence Nankam chipped in contribution through the phone, while Treasurer Julius Ashu dropped off required documentation on his way from the hospital with the sick son.

Done by Dr. Peter A. Fossungu
Outgoing Chair, GAC.

The only two cases of CGAM uncontroversial marriages that can be quickly given here are those of Bridget Fomenky in November 2007 and Jackson Acha Atam in May 2008. During the January 2006 review, there was a *Tetonistic* proposal (touching the birth/marriage *sociopackism*) requiring that new members of the association should serve a probation period of three months before they can qualify to receive the statutory allocation for child assistance as described in the by-laws. What followed the proposition was quite lively and passionate. This suggestion was rejected by the Najemerite BRC itself. But the president (perhaps still feeling the 2005 *Teton-Claude* embarrassment – see Fossungu, 2015b: 150-52) took the floor and harped on the need for a probation period. Anung Wilson (Note that I usually leave the order of names as they are when I am directly or substantially reproducing the Minutes, like here) was of the opinion that a probation period should only affect new members who had been living in Canada for a while and not those just coming in for the first time. Karen Najeme drew the attention of members to the negative implications of such a suggestion to the group's image. She further suggested that the allocations stipulated by the bylaws be made available to new members once they join the group, irrespective of how long they have been living in Canada. This idea was supported by Peter Fossungu who said that a member should be a member! The house supported that a member should be a member! The S-G failed here (unlike the video camera) to properly record an important statement that preceded this generally acclaimed 'a member is a member' position. It is important because that is precisely what opened the sleeping eyes and led to consensus on the point. Fossungu's argument leading to it was that we should rather *stick to stricter entry scrutiny* rather than allowing someone to come in as a member and then turn around to treat them differently from other members in terms of rights and obligations.

Another proposal that was received called for three designated members to attend a born-house on behalf of all members. Denis Alem, a member of the BRC, explained that the reason for the proposal was to save money. This plan was rejected by the house, which adopted the donation of $200.00 to the event while women bring food and men come along with drinks to the occasion. This certainly ties in well with the founding idea of sharing in members' joy and grief, the monetary amount being just a token. This *Tokenism* again! That would be Eveline Awemu Ibeagha (in *Adhoc Democracy*) hating *tokenism*, not me. It seems to me that a lot of people have refused (deliberately or otherwise) to learn that you cannot have your cake and eat it (*foolerrandism*); or is it 'eat it' before 'have it'? Whatever way it is put, the important thing is that the *foolerrandism* lesson (if there is any message at all in the CGAM) has been woefully jettisoned; and this by the numerous CGAM administrations. But the *Fifolefacist* era (shortened to *Fifolefacism*) wins the trophy for *politickerizing* not only with CGAM institutions (GAC, GWFC) but also with the social packages. This makes you begin to wonder if *wilanungalism* (the Anung *resigaspensionisn* charge) is not a valid thesis, or whether it is the dictator-fear syndrome that is driving this guy (with such exceptional organizational qualities) to the tree-*topperism* business?

The Dictator-Fear Syndrome or Egyptian-*Kingism*?

In 2008 the GAC interestingly was composed of four members – two ex-presidents (Paul Ayah and Peter Fossungu) and two founding members (Valentine Usongo and Walter Ndonkeu) – with all four being founding members! Wouldn't you expect that such a body was ably suited to handle whatever constitutional issues that landed before it? Well, you will soon find out on what side your guess fell. On June 26, 2008 the CGAM president, in a communication (titled '*Referral of Constitutional Matters*') to the GAC, pleaded:

Dear Members of Goodwill Advisory Council (GAC),

On behalf of the executive, I write to refer three proposals for amendments of the constitution and/or by-laws from some members of Goodwill. As you know, it was agreed during the October 2007 meeting that such matters shall be referred to GAC for recommendations. Below are the proposals:

1. Effective from the meeting following birth, the nursing mother should be given three months of maternity leave during which she will not be expected to pay for entertainment only. She will however, pay for all other social packages. (Proposal from Hervege).

2. Revise the policy on the payment of marriage checks; from when the spouse arrives [in] Canada to as soon as the member is married. She thinks that she has been denied this right to her marriage check as a member, reason why she has not been making her contributions. (Proposal from Vivian Beng)

3. Current contributions for social packages, especially birth and marriages need to be revised. (Proposal from Jacobine)

4. Procedure for filling a vacant executive office before the end of mandate (Executive proposal)

We shall appreciate if you can handle these issues and inform us before the July thematic meeting so that they can be tabled for adoption.

Best regards, Fidelis Folifac, President, Goodwill.

Of course, I must state that, from the logic of the *April-Fool Democracy* (discussed in Fossungu, 2015b: chapter 4 – the Paulayahist cabinet), the Fifolefacist administration should have simply made it clear to the members concerned that they should make their proposals to the next BRC that was scheduled to operate a few months later. That is precisely what you would expect from a genuine talker of the respect of the constitution or straight-talker.[45] It seems to be so easy

---

[45] To grasp this point well, listen, for example, to Momany fossungupalogizing to his sister and her husband after talking on the phone with the husband regarding the 'police-family thesis' letter you have already read above. This message to "Dear James and Marie-Claire" was written on April 1, 1999:

I want to thank you for the phone call and talk of today (April 1). It seems you guys left the house immediately you dropped the receiver of the phone. It is only unfortunate I didn't know Marie-Claire was also present at home. I thereafter called her place of work before realizing she was at home. Calling home to talk to her, nobody was there and no answering machine came up. So I couldn't leave any message; and, therefore, this note comes to say what I wanted to say.

Well, Marie-Claire, listening to James a few minutes ago, I realize I should have called rather than writing as I did. But I just want you both to know that I should not have written that letter (mean as it is) if I do not hold you very dear to heart. Otherwise, it wouldn't have meant a thing at all to me hearing those stories – founded or not.

I would also want to let you know you have proven to be the kind of guys I have always thought you are (and I am hardly ever wrong about some of these things) by the way you have handled this whole confusion and misunderstanding. I just wish I didn't lose my cool as I did, and that Scholastica too could handle the nasty note I also sent [to] her the way you have. There is evidently some gross misunderstanding and I wish we could be able to sit down all four of us together and put things straight.

to talk the talk when one wants power at all costs. Nevertheless, the GAC referral was also an option through which to wash-off hands like the Egyptian king who could have freed Jesus on the spot but preferred to do the hand washing. Is that not what tree-*topperism* is all about? Doing it while someone else takes the blame, clearly defines it. This is what I call the dictator-fear syndrome but which other critics would prefer to style the fear of politics.

CGAMers have so much faith in the GAC as an institution capable of efficiently resolving near-intractable constitutional and other issues. Just listen to what they actually think to comprehend what I am trying so hard to tell you. '*To The Goodwill Advisory Council (GAC)*' is the title of an interesting communication from S-G Enongene Ekwe, sent on October 3, 2011 to "Dear Members of the GAC". The S-G passionately indicated that:

> I write on the request of the Goodwill General Assembly (GGA) to notify you of its need for your service.
>
> For 1.5 years running, the assets and financial records of the association have not been audited. In trying to improve on this situation, the GGA so[ugh]t to identify a

---

Sometimes it just has to take more than one head to see certain things clearly.

Once more, thanks for the call and chat. I am very relaxed now. You wouldn't have been shocked by my note, let alone call in regard of it, if you didn't care. I wouldn't have written it if I wasn't shocked and did not care. I just don't know how to fill my mind with bad thoughts about people, especially those I hold dearly to heart. I would now completely undo that note if I could. After listening to James today, I have already taken back everything I frantically said; and am asking you both to let it go. But if you cannot let it go, I understand you are entitled to that.

Sincerely, P.A. Fossungu.

competent group of individuals to audit the long standing records. 20 of the 22 GGA members present in the September meeting voted for the GAC to perform this role. This notice is therefore an official summon of the GAC to the October 8th thematic meeting. The GGA specifies that your attendance of this meeting should be treated as mandatory, cognizance of the fact that this will be the last meeting before elections (November) and subsequent power transition. The GGA trusts that your wealth of experience, ingenuity and dedication to Goodwill's course [cause?] are second to none in guiding this association through turbulent waters. So, please, be sure that the GGA counts on your personal presence at this meeting.

In fact, the membership would have every reason to look up to this body that is supposed to be non-partisan and 'all-knowing'. Its creation having come in a year of serious crisis would confirm this stance. From the 13 October 2007 GGA Minutes produced by Interim S-G Anung, we clearly learn this: "During the extra-ordinary meeting held on the October 6, 2007 (see the attachment of minutes of this meeting [which are attached nowhere that this blind me and you could see]) an advisory committee was created, pending approval and adoption by the General Assembly. Members of this committee are the founding fathers of Goodwill, namely Peter Fossungu, Valentine Usongo and Walter Tita and by default all ex-presidents of Goodwill which led to the inclusion of Paul Ayah[46]. They are solely responsible for Constitutional matters and the by-laws. A member of this

---

[46] But Paul Ayah is also a founding member, or isn't he? For more details on the thirteen founders, see Fossungu (2015b: 5).

committee cannot be an executive member! This committee was adopted by the [October 2007] General Assembly." As you already know, the sitting president is now also a member, following a 2008 amendment. The essential question is: Does the GAC actually live up to expectations? We will find that out together using (1) their in-house dealings concerning the issues referred to the institution by the Executive Bureau and (2) the fate of their recommendations in the GGA.

The GAC's Intra-Exchanges and Recommendations: One versus Three?

When the GAC got the 4-point referral, the then chair of GAC was Peter Ateh-Afac Fossungu who on June 29, 2008 communicated his ideas to the three colleagues (Paul Takha Ayah, Valentine Usongo, Walter Tita Ndonkeu), making it clear that his belief is "that the GAC must always look at 'proposals' for changing laid down rule[s] of this Association with a level head, detached from all emotion, with the best interest of Goodwill being our sole measuring rod." And that it was in that respect that he wanted to share his thought with the others before they met "concerning the four 'proposals' referred to us." He then addressed the referred points as follows:

1. **Maternity Leave**. This same issue came up in one of our Dec. Constitutional Revising Assemblies (Paul's Presidency) held in the Caribbean Paradise. The discussions were very lively and heated but in the end, to eschew the opening of a floodgate of exceptions (e.g. paternity leave, sick leave, travel leave, etc), the

current position was taken. It was probably to mitigate the hardship to families that, at the same session, the reduced Family (Couple) Amount for entertainment was introduced and adopted. Maybe we should all take a keen look at the session in question (that is, the video of the deliberations). This is thus not a new issue to Goodwill and perhaps we will save ourselves some time if new members are adequately put up to date regarding Goodwill history and developments.

2. **Marriage Cheques**. The clause in the Regulations regarding marriages contracted out of Montreal was, again, adopted in order to avoid abuse. (The deliberations are also on tape.) We are not here saying that all such persons are not in fact married, but I think what we have in place is reasonable and should be maintained. We must avoid making and remaking our laws following the presentation of particular or specific cases or else we will soon have no known laws at all. (As a footnote, I must say that even Equity will not be on the Petitioner's side as she is now unjustifiably not up-to-date with her contributions to Goodwill and to other Goodwillers. You simply cannot come knocking at the door of Equity with dirty hands.)

3. **Birth and Marriage Packages**. I would like to rest my case here until I am told what is wrong with the current regulation and practice, as well as what the Petitioner is proposing in lieu [of the

existing policy]. However, if what I heard in Gatineau (that these are too frequent, meanwhile some of us are no longer having children, nor marrying) is the foundation of this "proposal", then I would want to remind us that we cannot be truly rejoicing in Goodwill's near-universality and exponential increase in membership without also being prepared to assume the full scale of the responsibility that inevitably accompanies this kind of membership. In a gathering such as ours, to actively support a rule in place only because we hope to personally gain from it is, to say the least, highly immature and eccentric. This Association was created by, and for, mature and good willing people; not [for] immature and self-centred people. The latter have no place in Goodwill Montreal and, thank God, there is adequate and appropriate provision for leaving should we find that we are in the wrong place.

4. **Procedure for Filling Vacant Executive Posts**. Let us have the Executive Bureau prepare a section to be added to the portion dealing with The Executive which will provide that "following any vacancy in the Executive Bureau, the General Assembly shall, at its earliest session, following such vacancy, conduct special elections to fill the post".

This is what I think about the issues. What about you?
PAF

You would expect that an august group like this one would be able to brainstorm on the issues before actually meeting physically to just to fine-tune the problems. Not so with the 'Hounourable GAC' of the CGAM. The only one who responded to the last question was Valentine Usongo who wrote on June 30 as follows:

Hi President: I got your mail concerning the four point agenda which you have already given your opinion on some of the issues. I wish to state that by you making the point "This Association was created by, and for, mature and good willing people; not immature and self-centred people" is completely out of touch. Financial resources are not the same for individuals and the policy of handing cheques to people when they have kids is financially unsustainable. By you saying that "The latter have no place in Goodwill Montreal and, thank God, there is adequate and appropriate provision for leaving should we find that we are in the wrong place" to me sounds arrogant and is not the best way to look into a legitimate concern.

As one of the founding fathers of this association I have been personally contributing and it has never bothered me, and it will never bother that I contribute. However that doesn't mean that I should not sympathise with others who complain that the contributions are too much. The fact that we can contribute all the time and others complain that the contributions are too much does not mean that they should leave the group if they cannot meet up. In the group they [sic] are students and others with limited finances and I think it is worth looking into this. Births and marriages are planned and warrants [sic] no contribution. Unexpected situations like death warrant[] contributions. In any case, I will try and make it for [M]onday next week just inform me of the time. [H]ave a great week.

[V]alentine

The question I keep asking is: Where were these guys when the same GGA was voting for these measures in January? Busy with their Heineken bottles? The four GAC members had a hard time agreeing on a date to convene that was good for all, but eventually met on July 9, 2008. From the pre-convention exchanges above, I would not need to point out to you that it was clearly a one-against-three match. But the following compromised recommendations were jointly arrived at and sent to the Executive Bureau only after each concerned GACer had read, made the necessary corrections, additions, etc (where need be[47]):

---

[47] On Friday, July 11, 2008 Peter Fossungu (duly copying Ayah, Usongo, and Ndonkeu) sent "Recommendations Reached On Matters Referred to The GAC" to Mr. President, stating: "In this correspondence you will find the Recommendations that the GAC is to present and defend tomorrow at the meeting. By sending this to you beforehand we are just trying to help your Bureau prepare, if that is the aim at this point, the required legislation that could be tabled for adoption after the GAC's presentation. The Recommendations are as follows:...."

RECOMMENDATIONS OF THE GOODWILL ADVISORY COMMITTEE (GAC)

On 26 June 2008, the Executive of Goodwill Montreal, through the President, wrote (viewing the agreement during the October 2007 meeting that such matters be referred to the GAC for recommendations) to refer three petitions for amendments of the constitution and/or by-laws from some members of Goodwill, as well as one emanating from the Executive. The petitions that the GAC received were:

1) Effective from the meeting following birth, nursing mothers should be given three months of maternity leave during which time they will not be expected to pay for entertainment at monthly meetings.

2) Revise the policy on the payment of marriage checks (for marriages contracted out of Montreal) from "when the other spouse arrives [in] Canada" to "as soon as the member is married".

3) Revise current contributions for social packages, especially regarding birth and marriages.

4) Lay down the procedure for filling a vacant executive office that comes up before the end of mandate.

The GAC, meeting in Plenary Session on 9 July 2008, took a seasoned and informed look at these petitions and came to the conclusion that the entire Idea of Social Packages, Entertainment, and Contributions in our Regulations needed major overhaul so as to keep up with the exponential explosion in Goodwill Membership. The general consensus has been that the aforementioned items have simply become too burdensome, financially, to Goodwillers and something must have to be done to alleviate the load. The principal issue before the GAC then has not been whether or not to remedy the escalating situation but *how* to go about doing so. The problems raised here are not new issues in the sense that our Regulations in place do cover them. The Constitution, for example, that was duly adopted by the General Assembly in January 2008 clearly spells out the rules in their regard and even goes further to make the document good for one calendar year. Are we now to go ahead and scrap off or refashion some of these rules in mid-year simply because their due application has become too financially burdensome to members?

The GAC, after a careful examination, does think that we can do so: provided we do not in the course of doing so cause undue hardship to the general membership or even a cross-section of it. In a nutshell, the GAC's enterprise here has been that of striking the right and reasonable balance between (1) the rights of the *general membership* not to be overwhelmed by too many and frequent financial contributions toward the well planned and foreseeable acts/events (such as births and marriages) of other members and (2) the rights of some members (also included in the *general membership* mentioned above) who had to benefit (in the same way as others have already done) from the law as it currently is. It has been in its utmost desire to see justice and equity done to all Goodwillers that the GAC has come up with the following Recommendations, recommendations that we do hope do put all Goodwillers in a Win-Win Position (Illustrations to be given during presentation):

A. <u>ENTERTAINMENT</u>:

(i) Monthly entertainment charge shall be ten dollars (10.00$) per member per meeting.

(ii) This amount shall be paid in this manner. Each payment shall cover at least three meetings.

(iii) Nursing mothers are exempted from paying this charge for three successive meetings, effective from the meeting following their giving birth.

B. <u>SINKING FUND</u>:

(i) Every member shall pay a fixed yearly amount of fifty dollars (50.00$) toward this Fund.

(ii) Payment of this amount shall be made by returning Members at the beginning of the year (January).

(iii) New Members being sponsored must include this amount as part of their application for membership before it can be examined.

C. <u>BIRTHS AND MARRAIGES</u>:

Social packages (cheques) given for these two events shall be scrapped off completely, come December 31, 2008.

Until then, these are the refashioned rules [that] have to apply.

(i) Cheques shall be given for births in the amount of two hundred dollars (200.00$) per member.

(ii) Cheques shall be given for marriages in the amount of two hundred dollars (200.00$) per member

(iii) All outstanding marriages have to be taken care of before the end of the year (2008), irrespective of the presence of the other spouse in Montreal (for those contracted out of Montreal).

D. <u>DEATHS</u>:

Cheques shall be given for deaths (of the covered relationships) in the amount of one thousand five hundred dollars (1500.00$) per member.

E. <u>FILLING VACANCY</u>:

The procedure for filling vacancy in the Executive shall be as follows.

(i) Elections to fill the position shall be conducted in the next meeting following the vacancy.

(ii) In case no candidate(s) make themselves available for the elections in (i) above, the President shall appoint, on an ad hoc basis at every meeting, someone to fill the post until a new bureau is duly elected at end of the mandate concerned.

For The GAC

Chairperson

Dr. Peter A. Fossungu

Toying with the GAC Recommendations: *Doublesidism* or Stark Failure of Duty?

You would expect that, after this meticulous exercise, the issue was laid to rest. Not exactly so with *politickerizers* who always want to please everybody in politics by playing *doublesidism*. Another name for the game, if I may draw from my own family again, is backstabbing reclusiveness. I have found dealing with my siblings of the household who keep everything inside them worse than with my gregarious and very disrespectful brother, Joseph, who you already know well. But I will here stay focused on the CGAM. What was the need of referring these issues to the GAC if a member would thereafter ask for a vote on any single one of them and the same Executive Bureau allows that to be done? That is exactly how the same emotions you witnessed above being expressed inside the GAC itself tickled down to the more unruly GGA and had the birth and marriage social packages scrapped completely right in front of about six mothers (and their husbands) who were not only expecting their babies soon but also expecting fair and guaranteed treatment. These are persons who had contributed to others' full packages that same year (to leave out all their other years of membership). You get the real sense of it from the Financial Secretary's announcement for that same July scrapping-off session. 'JULY *Financial Contributions & Social Assistance payments*' was Pius Esambe Etube's July 11, 2008 communication to 'Dear members' who had to know that

This month, individual financial statements have not been sent out. Kindly refer to your June statement. In addition to what we had to pay in June we have another birth. The Tanwani family will also be a beneficiary of $700 birth assistance, for which every member has to contribute $9 plus normal $15 monthly fee. Thus your payments required in July meeting would be as follows:

- *Members who paid their contributions in June (up to date @100%): will have to pay $24 each ($15 for entertainment and $9 for Tanwani family)*
- *Others: Your June payment less any portion paid plus $24 ($15 for entertainment and $9 for Tanwani family)*

We have to issue out cheques worth a total sum of about $3000. So far only about $400 has been contributed. If we are unable to contribute we will have no option than to issue cheques in terms of date of the event. I wish to appeal to you all as usual to go the extra mile so that we can honour our commitment to members who are beneficiaries to social assistance payments.

Members should be aware that some members still owe outstanding balances from 2007. By implication these members have not paid for any assistance payment contributions or entertainment in 2008. In brief, for six months they have not been contributing. Maintaining these names in our financial records puts the association on a deficit because we will never realize the expected amount for any form of assistance. I humbly submit to the [G]eneral Assembly to make a pronouncement on this issue.

My regards to all and see you in the meeting tomorrow.

Financial Secretary, Pius Etube [emphasis is original]

As you can see therefore, these near-term moms never got even the *quarter-package* (200/700) suggested in the GAC recommendations (which I personally fought to secure against the three giant throwing- everything-out option). It was horrifying to watch and be part of this heartless drama. The more dishearteningly so when you must have witnessed the joy and jubilation that all those *nonoselfistic* hypocrites expressed after the illicit (and I would even say conspired) vote. But let's not talk heartlessness and conspiracy until we hear of the same CGAM president authorizing and justifying payments of marriage packages to his "friends" a day or so later. On July 14, 2008 the president wrote his *'2006-2007 Social Package'* message to "Dear All", making clear that:

I am cc ing Vivian Beng, Charles Nkwenti and members of Goodwill Advisory Council this email for the purpose of accountability and responsiveness in service delivery.

Following the new policies of Goodwill, voted during the July thematic meeting on Saturday 12, 2008, Goodwill is required to honour (pay out) any outstanding social package before the end of this year.

The case (marriage) of Vivian Beng has been outstanding from 2006. Following the policy in force

172

then, her check will be issued from Goodwill's account. Please Vivian contact the Fin. Sec. for your social check.

Charles Nkwenti, also informed me, after the meeting on Saturday, of his case (marriage) as outstanding for 2007. Following the 2007 policy, members need to contribute for this. I request that Goodwillers be adequately and immediately informed of this and the contribution needed to meet this obligation.

Lastly, please Fin. Sec. send a general email to Goodwillers asking if there is any member with an outstanding social package for 2006 and 2007.

Thanks for your prompt action.

This talk of "following the policy in force", in my view, was seriously flawed and outrageous, and could only expose the hidden motive behind all the 'referral' to the GAC in the first place. *Egyptian-kingism*, call it. The GAC recommendations, as I earnestly explained in the GGA before the fatal vote, were to be voted on as a package. That means that the entire thing had to be accepted or rejected. Because a lot of people were just targeting the heavily pregnant women and their families, no attention was paid to fairness. Everything was scrapped off the books therefore. Thus, with the immediate and subsequent new talk of actually paying out for marriage packages,[48] Peter Ateh-Afac

---

[48] It is important that I give you here the complete Minutes of the October 2008 GGA on the non-issue that exposes a lot of deception and *doublesidism* or *egytian-kingism*:
1) **Case of Two Outstanding Marriages:**
<u>**Case 1 Mr. Charles Nkwenti**</u>
The president reported to the GGA that, Mr. Charles Nkwenti approached him about his marriage-benefits for the year 2007. The matter was discussed at the executive meeting but there were no records

pertaining to Mr. Nkwenti's marriage. The executive resolved that Goodwill owes Mr. Nkwenti no liability. The matter was then brought to the GGA for sanctioning.

The debate was opened with some members wanting to know when Mr. Nkwenti's wife arrived in Montreal and also sought to know what the by-laws says on the procedures for reporting marriages within Goodwill. Some members reiterated that, the married [sic] and birth assistance packages were stopped in July 2008 and Goodwill had agreed to pay only benefits that were pending and officially recorded.

The president replied that, Mr. Nkwenti's wife is now in Montreal and he got married in 2007 when membership contribution was in force. He also responded that, there was a procedural void in the by-laws on how social events were officially reported to Goodwill. The president also went ahead to cite jurisprudence in the case of Felicia Tatuh while emphasising that Vivian Mbeng's case was different and could therefore not serve as a reference to Mr. Nkwenti's request.

On the other hand, some members held the opinion that; Mr Nkwenti deserved to receive the marriage package. They also argued that it wasn't Mr. Nkwenti's fault if there were no records for he did inform the former executive and was only waiting for the wife to arrive to Montreal as stipulated in the former by-laws. However, members agreed that, Mr. Nkwenti's case is a special one since there was lack of records and continuity from the previous executive, necessitating the need for documented proof to settle the matter.

In a bid to have a clearer view on the matter, the president verified Mr. Charles Nkwenti's financial standing of which it was ok and later moved that, the GGA should vote on the following points:-

1) The executive to verify with Mr. Charles Nkwenti if he got married after becoming member of Goodwill. If yes then Goodwill will proceed to pay him.

2) Since Vivian Mbeng was paid then Mr Charles Nkwenti has to be paid.

Thirteen members voted in favour for point number one while three members voted for point number two and nine members abstained. At this juncture, the President withdrew the previous position of the executive of not paying and concluded that, the executive will verify point number one as indicated by the majority and members will be informed via the group's email.

Case 2 Mr. Calep Nyambi

The president reported to the GGA the case of Mr Calep Nyambi who also approached him about his marriage package since he got married slightly before the date some social packages were scraped but

Fossungu 'went on the rampage' with his masterpiece titled
"'PENDING SOCIAL PACKAGES': TOYING WITH
THE GAC RECOMMENDATIONS" that hit the CGAM
airwaves on November 2, 2008. Here is it entirely:

Dear Goodwillers,

Permit me to take a few minutes of your weekend to
talk about these scrapped "social packages" that are now
still 'pending'. I have always indicated that when, in a
group like ours, we cannot learn to apply laid down rules
across the board without considering our personal
sentiments towards those affected or to be affected, we
will forever remain on the dance-floor of Eko Roosevelt's
GO-FOR-BEFORE-FOR BACK.

To make comprehension of the matter easier, I have
taken the pains to attach here the entire GAC
Recommendations, most of which were jettisoned during

---

never informed Goodwill. The Financial secretary was called upon to
verify his financial position vis-à-vis the by-laws. It was realised that, Mr
Calep Nyambi still owes more than 3 months of contributions. The
President resolved that, per Goodwill's by-laws the Association owes no
dime to Mr. Caleb Nyambi; a decision which was unanimously approved
by the GGA.

Case of Mrs Nathalie Nchotu
This was not on the agenda for the day but the president reported
that, the Treasury officer called him on the day of the thematic meeting to
inform him that, Mrs. Nathalie Nchotu also got married before those
social benefits were scraped and was waiting for her husband to arrive
thus will also need to be paid. The President informed the GGA that,
Goodwill was not informed officially that she got married though her
financial position was up to date. The president called upon the GGA to
take a decision on the matter. The GGA agreed that, Mrs. Nathalie
Nchotu's case should also be verified as with the case of Mr Charles
Nkwenti.

At this point, the president told the GGA that, although births and
marriages have been scraped, it is important to have a clear procedure that
members may use to report events.

the meeting at which they were presented. During the October meeting, the issue of "pending marriages social packages" was high on the agenda. Despite overwhelming and preponderant evidence that indicated that this was a non-issue, the matter was put to a 'pay or not' vote. And we all know the results of that vote, not [to] mention the sizeable number of abstentions. Putting the scrapped matter back onto the centre place of the October meeting's agenda was premised on the fact that the Goodwill Advisory Council (GAC) had recommended that "All outstanding marriages have to be taken care of before the end of the year (2008), irrespective of the presence of the other spouse in Montreal (for those contracted out of Montreal)." True to say, the GAC made that recommendation. But that clause was not standing, and was never meant to stand on its own and to have treated it as such is to misconstrue the GAC Recommendations on social packages in regard of Births and Marriages.

Both events are covered by Section C of the Recommendations. It is only normal and logical that subsections C(i) to C(iii) can only flow from the major premise, namely, that "Social packages (cheques) given for these two events shall be scrapped off completely, come December 31, 2008." And what follows is even more graphical to the point at hand: Until 31 December 2008 when there was to be complete scrapping of these births and marriages "packages", THESE REFASHIONED RULES HAVE TO APPLY: (i) to (iii). Subsections C(i) to C(iii) of the GAC's Recommendations were to have any force of rule only if the Births and

Marriages "social packages" were maintained until 31 December 2008. It is that simple.

Since the [Goodwill] General Assembly [GGA] decided there and then (and with a lot of uncalled for sentiments towards the families of the many heavily pregnant ladies) to scrap these packages, why are we still now talking of "pending social packages for marriages"? As most of you can now realize, all what the [Goodwill] General Assembly was purportedly voting on during the last meeting had no foundation. Null and void is the phrase that the law uses to describe it. When it is scrapped it is scrapped. What is scrapped is scrapped. The only way to come back to these scrapped social packages will, perhaps, be to tell us of "Pending Births and Marriages Packages" and these must have to extend to all past ones (since the scrapping) as well as to all births and marriages that will occur until 31 December 2008 because, essentially, the question boils down to: Did we scrap these packages or did we not? Dr. Peter A. Fossungu

Of course, you wouldn't expect that those persons *politickerizingly* thinking that Fossungu was personally stepping on their toes would remain silent here. One of such doubtful beneficiaries was Charles Nkwenti Minjo.[49] Minjo went on 'the attack' on the same day (November 2), stating:

---

[49] Illicit because most of these people were hovering around the CGAM but were in fact of the Najeme breakaway faction called UNICAM. Here is the CGAM president's message to both Charles Minjo and Hans Najeme (copying CGAM) on Thursday, July 2, 2009 6:15:45 PM:
Mr. President and CEO
UNICAM Group

Dear Brothers,

On the occasion of events making the first anniversary celebration of UNICAM Group, I write to wish you, members of UNICAM Group as well as well-wishers a very fruitful celebration. In my personal capacity and as President of the Cameroon Goodwill Association of Montréal, I am delighted to note that as a people, our diversity should be a source of our strength in fostering the capacity and productivity of the Cameroonian community in Canada. To this effect, I have no doubts that this first anniversary celebration of UNICAM Group will be a true reflection of our diversity and dynamism.

Be assured, Mr. President and CEO, that Goodwill shares in every moment of this celebration in accordance with her commitment to a fruitful collaboration with all sister associations.

Accept, Mr. President and CEO, the expression of my highest esteem.

Best wishes of the first anniversary celebration
Fidelis Folifac
President, Goodwill.

Who would convince me that in July 2008 (let alone October same year) Fidelis Folefac did not clearly know where his friend Minjo stood? You just have to listen attentively to a secessionist talking *unity* to *four-eyesismatically* understand the science of doublesidism. Charles Nkwenti Minjo wrote back on Friday, July 3, 2009 5:50:15 PM:

Mr. President,

Thank you for your kind words and for the continuous hand of friendship and support you and the members of Goodwill have extended not only to UniCam Group but other groupings in Montreal.

Our celebration falls within the context of a realization of a vision, one set forth to better our livelihoods here in Canada and back home. Driven by a commitment to succeed, and encouraged by the community as a whole, UniCam has proven that united there is much we as a community can achieve in a host of profitable ventures our new country offers. Thus, we not only celebrate one year of existence, but the birth of a Vibrant Company, **UNICAM SHIPPING AND MOVING.**

I want to use this opportunity to thank you, Mr. President and your Executives and all members of Goodwill for opening up the community to the Authorities of the City LaSalle, because through you we have been able to get some material assistance towards our anniversary celebrations.

As we cement our bond, be it through associations or business, we ask you to remain committed, as you have been to the growth of our community. **I also ask all Goodwillers and all members of our**

This is ridiculous and divisive as most of you[r] lengthy and controversial pronouncement be it on the floor of the meeting or on this medium of communication.

I think with all fairness, we are honouring all the outstanding marriages and or births that preceded the enactment [of] this new bylaw(s), so ta[l]king about sentiments goes a long way to show [how] biased you[r] judgment is. Don't think am saying this because I was one of the beneficiaries. The GAC recommendations were not meant to be embraced in its entirety by the General Assembly and we should learn to accept decisions arrived at by a democratic vote.

---

community to patronize our young business by shipping with us to Cameroon and anywhere in the world.

Thank you very much,

Charles Nkwenti

President UniCam [capitals and bold are original]

And here enters Hans Najeme, the well-known *doublesidist*, even to the ACC (Association of Cameroonians in Canada): who wants to be reminded only by me of the Hans-Libai secret sabotaging communication that mistakenly reached all ACClist recipients? His reply to his CGAM partner-in-arms, which came in a day before Minjo's, read:

Mr. President,

On behalf of the Company, I wish to express our appreciation for your thoughtful wishes. I can assure you that with the relationship already established between your Association Goodwill and the Company (Unicam Group Inc), we look forward for a vibrant community here in Canada. The celebration of our first anniversary marks the transition of our Investment club into a full-fledged company thanks to Cameroonians like you who have demonstrated support for this project.

We look forward to a cordial business relationship with Goodwill.

Long live our Community

Hans Najeme

CEO

Unicam Group Inc.

179

Just hear some of them! Why didn't they accept that democratic vote rather than revisit and change decisions arrived at by a democratic vote in January? Why did the same guy here not accept the democratic vote of the December 2007 elections because of which he broke away? You must still remember Minjo as the first writer after the 2007 elections results – see Fossungu (2015b: 161-162). Of course, *Democracy-as-I-see fit*, that is it. Yet, *Fifolefacism* is one CGAM administration that prides itself on so many good governance factors, including 'accountability, transparency, answerability and the taking of responsibility for our actions' whereas the reality points to the idea that they are solely interested in putting the last nail on the coffin of the association or family: in the same way as Massachusetts and Texas did to DOMA's sarcophagus?

Chapter 5

Welcome To Judicial Homonista: Africa Keenly Watching As Massachusetts And Texas Hammer The Final Nail In Doma's Coffin?

A constitution is, in fact, and must be regarded by the judges, as a fundamental law. It therefore belongs to them to ascertain its meaning, as well as the meaning of any particular act proceeding from the legislative body. If there should happen to be an irreconcilable variance between the two, that which has the superior obligation and validity ought, of course, to be preferred; or, in other words, the Constitution ought to be preferred to the statute, the intention of the people to the intention of their agents (Alexander Hamilton, Federalist N° 78).

The fears of conservative politicians peaked in 2003, when the courts struck twice: the U.S. Supreme Court ruled in *Lawrence v. Texas* that state homosexual sodomy laws are unconstitutional, while the Supreme Judicial Court of Massachusetts in *Goodridge* ordered state officials to issue marriage licenses to same-sex couples (Liu and Macedo, 2005: 211). As the U.S. Senate debates on the FMA (Federal Marriage Amendment) have shown, "Legislators and their staffs on Capitol Hill seem to lack both the capacity and the motivation to advance a morally perfectionist case against same-sex partnerships" (Liu and Macedo, 2005: 214). This perceived deficiency plays well into the hands of those arguing in favour of judicial review, making the courts appear to be what some see as 'actually being the bastions of rationality'.

SSM and Sodomy Legalization: Are the Courts the Bastion of Rationality?

The first section here will look at the 2003 revolutionary cases of (1) *Goodridge* (in Massachusetts) in its match between procreation and commitment, and (2) *Lawrence* (from Texas to Washington) and its sodomy decriminalization. The second will then study the 2013 Supreme Court cases of *Windsor v. United States* (from New York) and *Hollingsworth v. Perry* (from California) that seek to assert the marriage-domain powers of the states.

Goodridge's the Procreation versus Commitment Argument and *Santorumizing Lawrence*'s Legalization of Sodomy: Who Is Fooling Who?

Before proceeding we need to consider the meaning and purposes of marriage. This institution is seen in many different ways. After all, to some critics, "marriage is mental and has to do with the way the concerned parties comport themselves, not just the piece of paper and ceremony evidencing the status. That could also explain the fact that I was physically away from my wife for four years but did not consider myself as being without a spouse" (Fossungu, 2015a: 11-12). To yet others, as already noted, it is well known that very few are the African men who get married without the central issue being to have children, explaining why "Without a child of his own for so long with Maria, Uncle Ngufor brought in his *njumba* who was carrying a baby for him."

(Fossungu, 2013c: 157). Because of the centrality of children to marriage in Africa, Uncle Ngufor got transformed from "a monogamist at heart to a polygamist of circumstances" (Fossungu, 2013c: 156). But in Neil Westbrook's study, "marriage", like in the DOMA, "refers to a traditional or historical view of marriage as a legal or religiously binding, lifelong, monogamous relationship between one man and one woman" (Westbrook, 2010: 8).

To leave out Utah's Mormonism in America,[50] the showing that the "DOMA Definition Equals Heterosexual Monogamy" (Fossungu, 2015a: 99-100), would raise some great amount of incomprehensibility in relation to polygamous Christian Africans.

> The important issue about the [DOMA] definition right now is that my father, for instance, was a staunch Catholic. The Catholic Church is one of the most outspoken religious denominations not only against SSM (same-sex marriage) but also polygamy. But just look at the number of wives he ended up with, simultaneously most of the time! Again, no big surprise to me, since I realize that he is a royal. The astonishing thing though relates to why these Africans cannot tell whoever is bringing their religion to them to either make it palatable with their (Africans') customs/cultures or disappear with it? (Fossungu, 2015a: 101; note omitted).

Why must Africans so easily lay down their customs in the face of foreign intruders? Wasn't the religious right of

---

[50] See Brian Robert Calfano, Amanda Friesen and Paul A. Djupe, "Mitigating Mormonism: Overcoming Religious Identity Challenges with Targeted Appeals" 46(3) *Political Science and Politics* (2013), 562-568.

Mormons to the practice of polygamy what was once litigated in *Reynolds v. United States* [98 U.S. 145 (1878)]? Could the prohibition of polygamy by the church and others (even in Cameroon that preaches *quadrijuralism*) therefore not simply be a question of what the critics see as 'religion deceiving through comforting'? That is, trying to impose one's limited worldview on everyone? Such an attitude would not be surprising to anyone who understands how Christian writers and other advocates always tend to presume to write/talk about 'all religions of the world' but "showed little inclination to treat non-Christian traditions with any sympathy" (Tweed, 1992: 440). Could the American courts also be guilty of this tendency? It would seem so, according to Buckley (2011: 323-24). He argues that the Supreme Court has used the same Blaine Amendment strategy in such cases as *Loke v. Davey* (2004), *Agostini v. Felton* (1997), *Mitchell v. Helms* (2000), and *Zelman v. Simmon-Harris* (2002). Even *Goodridge* appears not to be entire free of this bias.

Goodridge involved seven same-sex couples who had challenged the Massachusetts commonwealth's denial of marriage rights to them on numerous grounds. The justices found that the refusal to issue licenses essential for same-sex couples to marry served no rational state purpose and thus constituted a violation of the equal protection and due process provisions of the Massachusetts Constitution (Cunningham, 2005: 19). *Goodridge* thus also has the reputation of being "akin to a single shooting star in what was and continues to be a meteor shower of political action on this contentious issue in the United States" (Crehan, 2013: 13). The *Goodridge* Court stated that since pre-colonial days civil marriage has been a secular institution with no religious requirements attached. The Court elaborated upon the benefits as well as the burdens conferred by the state upon those who choose to marry, and thus welcome one of "life's momentous acts of self-definition" (Cunningham, 2005: 20). We have now clearly moved away from the procreation notion of marriage or what the critics regard as a sectarian definition of the institution. The prominence of the *Goodridge* decision is rightly deserved because "It was not just the amount that was written on the [SSM] subject that increased but the scope and breadth of the subjects of concern to the issue that saw a vast increase [after *Goodridge*]" (Crehan, 2013: 30-31).

As the court went on to indicate in *Goodridge*, hundreds of statutes relate to marriage and its benefits, many concerning property rights, such as tax laws, probate laws, protection from creditors, insurance provisions, and many more. Other areas of statutory rights include marital privilege, bereavement, child custody, and a panoply of other non-property related rights. The children of married couples enjoy legal, social, and economic protections. The Court stated that such reasons as well as the personal significance of marriage have cast the institution as a "civil right." 'Without the right to marry—or more properly, the right to choose to marry—one is excluded from the full range of human experience and denied full protection of the laws for one's 'avowed commitment to an intimate and lasting human relationship'" (Cunningham, 2005: 20). It has even been proven by some studies that

the categories of "child-raisers" and "opposite-sex couples" overlap poorly, not only because it is true that many opposite sex-couples cannot or will not have children, but also because, as the above figures illustrate, a great many same-sex couples do have children, either by adoption, reproductive technology, or from prior opposite-sex relationships or encounters. The same-sex marriage ban denies children living in same-sex households, some 2–8 million in number (Patterson 1995, 262), the benefits and protections of having married parents (Gerstmann, 2005: 218).

The *Goodridge* Court ruling was against the arguments of the Department of Public Health (numerous friendly groups, both pro- and anti-gay marriage, also filed briefs). The Department argued in favour of the role of marriage in procreation. But the Court found that it is commitment to each other, not procreation that is the essence of marriage. To rely on the fact that man and woman can procreate naturally and same-sex couples cannot, said the Court, "confers an official stamp of approval on the destructive stereotype that same-sex relationships are inherently unstable and inferior to opposite-sex relationships and are not worthy of respect" (Cunningham, 2005: 20). "Interestingly," Marshall Gram Crehan tersely notes, "the Attorney General was making the procreation argument to Chief Justice Margaret Marshall who despite being married for over 20 years had no children" (Crehan, 2013: 85). Some other family politics critics would see the stress put on the marriage certificate as not as important as the parties intentions, concluding that, "Official or not, I have posited already that marriage is more in what/how the parties to it feel, not simply the piece of paper evidencing it. It is a commitment to each other. That is clearly my take on marriage and family" (Fossungu, 2015a: 56).

The Massachusetts Court also found that the argument that two parent families of the opposite sex form the optimal arrangement for child rearing was unpersuasive; with the

Court rather stressing the changing nature of the family in American society, as well as the wide range of public benefits enjoyed by children in married families. The Court easily rejected the Department of Health's claim that limiting marriage to opposite-sex couples preserves scarce public resources. The majority also found that same-sex marriage is no threat to the fundamental value of marriage in the commonwealth, nor does it threaten the "natural" order of marriage, ordering Massachusetts city and town clerks to begin issuing marriage licenses to same-sex couples in 180 days, by 17 May 2004 (Cunningham, 2005: 20).

But wait a minute! Was that Chief Justice John Marshall talking? In view of the *Goodridge* order here, one may be wondering about the Marshall ruling in *Marbury* regarding mandamus being an unconstitutional expansion of courts' powers beyond what the constitution permits? To correctly answer this question, it must be borne in mind that "law, whatever its origins, is fundamentally connected to the social and political life from which it arises and which, in turn, it seeks to influence" (Bogart, 1994: ix). The answer to the quiz then resides in the fact that it was simply Chief Justice Marshall's clever way of not reducing the power and status of the judiciary in view of the context of the *Marbury* litigation, which was entirely different with the *Goodridge* Court.

Furthermore, some have questioned the rules that characterize marriage as being primarily about providing a stable environment for children. That being the case, then they hold that current rules on who may marry and who may not are poorly suited to this purpose. After all, they explain,

opposite-sex couples are allowed to marry whether or not they intend to, or are capable of, having children.

Some courts, including the Arizona court, have said that inquiries into the willingness or capacity of opposite-sex couples to bear children would violate their privacy. This is a difficult argument to sustain. First of all, there are some groups, such as, for example, very elderly women, who cannot bear children. Yet, it is inconceivable that any legislator who wished to keep his or her job would argue that, say, because their reproductive years are over women over the age of 80 should be banned from marriage and the legal and financial benefits it affords. Such a ban would not necessarily violate the constitutional doctrine of equal protection (the government is allowed to treat men and women differently when there are real differences in their situation), but would no doubt be seen as cruel and pointless. Why is it any less so when same-sex couples are banned from marriage for this reason? (Gerstmann, 2005: 218)

Santorumizing Lawrence: Who Is Fooling Who?

If the *Goodridge* rationale is seen as revolutionary, the word is also appropriately applied to *Lawrence*. In 2003 the U.S. Supreme Court in *Lawrence v. Texas* overturned its prior ruling in *Bowers v. Hardwick* (1986) by holding Texas' anti-sodomy laws to be unconstitutional. Justice Kennedy stated that "We think that our laws and traditions in the past half century ... show an emerging awareness that liberty gives substantive protection to adult persons in deciding how to conduct their private lives in matters pertaining to sex" (Crehan, 2013: 22). This was obviously a bomb shell to conservative values and also removed one firm argument against SSM. As a church official has recently regretted,

> In recent legislation in the District of Columbia, we are about to be forced to accept on our teaching faculties, Church staff and charitable services personnel those who live in a way that publically repudiates the teaching of the Church. The <u>Reproductive Health Non-Discrimination Act of 2014</u> (RHNDA) would deprive the Church of its right to ensure that those whom it entrusts to carry out its mission are faithful to its teachings on human life and sexuality. The law would instead force the Church and its ministries to hire and retain employees who obtain abortions, conceive via surrogates, and so on. Meanwhile, the <u>Human Rights Amendment of 2014</u> (HRAA) would require Catholic schools to formally recognize, endorse, and support student groups dedicated to promoting homosexual behavior. The new law says that for the Church to do otherwise in either case is unjust discrimination (Wuerl, 2015).

Yes. That is Texas' *Lawrence* still bulldozing around mercilessly. As a result of *Lawrence,* it is not at all clear why same-sex couples should be barred from marriage (Gerstmann, 2005: 218; Liu and Macedo, 2005: 212-213). Gerstmann writes,

> the Supreme Court cautioned against sweeping and simplistic accounts of history, and asserted that history and tradition are only the beginning points of any discussion of the basic rights of human beings. The Court did not specifically address the issue of same-sex

marriage; instead it simply noted that the case "does not involve whether the government must give formal recognition to any relationship that homosexual persons seek to enter." In dissent, Justice Scalia asserted that the Court's decision in *Lawrence* "leaves on pretty shaky grounds state laws limiting marriage to opposite-sex couples" (Gerstmann, 2005: 217-218).

The influence of *Lawrence* on *Goodridge* is clear from Chief Justice Margaret Marshall's statement:

It is a question the United States Supreme Court left open as a matter of Federal law in *Lawrence*, where it was not an issue. There, the Court affirmed that the core concept of common human dignity protected by the Fourteenth Amendment to the United States Constitution precludes government intrusion into the deeply personal realms of consensual adult expressions of intimacy and one's choice of an intimate partner. The Court also reaffirmed the central role that decisions whether to marry or have children bear in shaping one's identity" (cited in Crehan, 2013: 22).

The *Lawrence* ruling had led Senator Rick Santorum to declare that "If the Supreme Court says that you have the right to consensual [sodomitical] sex within your home, then you have the right to bigamy, you have the right to polygamy, you have the right to incest, you have the right to adultery. You have the right to anything" (cited in Liu and Macedo, 2005: 214). When you take freedom to the outer limits of liberty, I would argue, chaos ensures. Many commentators were critical of Santorum's "equating homosexual conduct with bigamy, polygamy, incest, and adultery, and the senator, a devout Catholic, quickly became a symbol of religious bigotry and intolerance" (Liu and Macedo, 2005: 214). But that, in my view, is probably the correct signification of the ruling, as uncomfortable to some as it is. The truth is that a lot of people don't like the truth. And the truth of *Lawrence* is one such bitter truth that easily puts off the untruthful and 'dollarocratic' public, thus making it hard for truthful politicians (if politics even has truth as constituting its definition) to be good politicians. I am obviously adopting *dollarocracy* from Nichols and McChesney.[51]

I agree with Russell that "[b]oth courts and legislatures are capable of being unreasonable and, in their different ways, self-interested. By providing a legislative counter-weight to judicial power the Canadian Charter establishes a prudent system of checks and balances which recognizes the fallibility of both courts and legislatures and gives closure to the decision of neither" (Russell, 1992: 481). Russell further furnishes some examples of courts' biased judgments, like restricting the free speech rights of workers in *B.C.G.E.U. v. British Columbia*, before concluding that "Professor Dale Gibson's article in the last issue of this journal [*Alberta Law Review*, vol. 29:1 (1991)] reveals other instances of judicial bias and self-interest in adjudicating public law issues" (Russell, 1992: 481). Let me add Montreal's family courts to this list of "other instances of judicial bias" for your pleasure.

Puzzling Family Politics in Montreal's Family High Court: Somewhere in *Africans and Negative Competition in Canadian Factories: Revamping Canada's Immigration, Employment,*

---

[51] John Nichols and Robert W. McChesney, *Dollarocracy: How the Money-and-Media Election Complex Is Destroying America* (New York: Nations Books, 2013).

and Welfare Policies? (2015: chapter 2), I described some
Canadian courts as 'Mechanical Courts'. This "controversial"
thesis was posited with particular reference to Ontario's
London Family High Court. Now, I want you to listen to
Momany's story in Montreal and tell me what you think about
Russell's charge. Momany has two children with his partner.
They separated in late January 2013. On January 30, 2013
there was a court order giving both of them shared custody,
with each party paying daycare for a child. On April 28, 2014
Momany's ex-partner went back to court asking for children
support from Momany who had gone to school in Ontario in
September 2013. The court maintained the shared custody
agreement intact while ordering the payment of children
support by Momany. That is, children support in addition to
also paying daycare for one child. Note also that this children
support is not calculated based on half-month – which is
normally supposed to be the case in shared custody - but full
month. It is all the handiwork of the woman's lawyer, not the
judge who merely validates it.

Being the gold-diggers that some of these ladies are,
Momany's ex-partner was still not satisfied and went back to
the court in January 2015 demanding full custody of the
children and children support. At this point, Momany also
made his own claim for full custody of the children without
asking for any court-ordered children support from his ex-
partner. The verdict of the case was set for March 6, 2015,
date at which Momany must have completed his schooling
and possibly returned to Montreal. Despite Momany's strong
arguments to the contrary, on 6 March 2015 the court
(mechanically, you would say?) accorded full custody of the
children to his ex-partner, giving him access rights and
ordering him to pay a lawyer-only-re-assessed children

support based on an imaginary annual earning (remember that Momany has just left school and still unemployed and job-hunting). This same court order goes on to mandate that Momany is still to continue paying one of the children's daycare! There is more and more and more and more.

I cannot actually discuss all the imponderables of this court's very faulty litigation politics here. It is a joke. But take a few examples. If Momany appeared in the Montreal court ten times for this same suit, it was before ten different judges, with most of them consequently not even knowing what the file before them consisted of, and having therefore to rely totally on what the lawyer for the woman was telling them. Not paying attention to whatever Momany had to say, perhaps because they did not see him as a lawyer or someone who could even know what was going on. It is even the woman's lawyer who calculated the support amount all the time and the judges simply imposed it in toto. It was a real drama on March 6, with Momany (who was representing himself) just being a spectator since the judge constantly shut him up (with "Don't argue with me or you'll be sorry!") whenever he tried to insist on raising an objection to the farce. Here then are some issues for your review. Is it normal for Momany to be paying children support to a *full custodian* of their children *and* still be additionally responsible for paying the daycare expenses of one of these children? Does the Montreal Family High Court actually understand what a decree of full custody means? Would Momany be violating the law or not: if (for instance) he stands in the way of his ex-partner's move to change the children's daycare provider?

Could the Massachusetts Chief Justice, Margaret Marshall, too possibly have been biased towards those who can easily procreate or have children that she has not had for over twenty years of heterosexual marriage? Countering the thesis of legislative irrationality and the urgent need for the courts to afford protection to minorities, one expert has stated:

Now, I have no doubt that legislative bodies can act unreasonably and fall under the sway of very repressive forces. In the 1950s we witnessed just that when McCarthyism held sway in the United States. We also witnessed then how ineffective that country's judicial guardians were in checking that repression. But more fundamentally, I would argue that a democracy which puts its faith as much in its politically active citizenry as in its judges to be the guardians of liberty is stronger than one that would endeavour to vest ultimate responsibility for liberty and fundamental rights exclusively in its judiciary (Russell, 1992: 485).

When courts do go too far in reordering society and there is too much untruthfulness going around, the minority can be just as harmful to rights and values of the majority as the majority may be to those of minorities. In such a situation, it becomes an uphill task for truth-tellers to prevail. Some critics have quoted Ponnuru as observing that Republicans face a dilemma criticizing decisions like *Goodridge* and *Lawrence* because "If the argument is made openly, and cast as a case for traditional sexual morals in general, a large part of the public will flinch. If the argument is made so as to single out gays, the logic vanishes" (Liu and Macedo, 2005: 214). For Senate Republicans debating the FMA, then, the lessons of *Lawrence* were political rather than legal. These lessons were epitomized by the experience of Senator Santorum and, for that matter, the Catholic Church whose stiff opposition to the *Goodridge* decision led the Church's critics to assert that

'The Church Is From Mars, The Court Is From Venus' (Cunningham, 2005: 21-23).

As some writers have observed, whereas once LGBT people had sought primarily the right to be left alone, as a result of such rulings as *Goodridge* and *Lawrence* they are now increasingly demanding the right to be recognized as equals. The recent shift toward marriage, the experts assert, probably would not have occurred for another decade without these legal victories. Although efforts to protect gay and lesbian families—including domestic partners benefits and adoption rights—gathered steam in the 1990s, marriage was only rarely explicitly promoted by the movement's leaders (Egan and Sherrill, 2005: 230). Crehan (2013: 22) then theorizes that "The Supreme Court in deciding *Lawrence* did more than strike down irrelevant laws but paved the way for further gains in the area of gay rights." I would go further and adopt from Cunningham's Mar-Venus thesis and similarly posit that, with *Lawrence*, we can now pull the Wallersteiner Curtain away and see that it is Canada which is the real melting-pot instead of America whose melting-pot stance "seems to be true *only* to its Blacks whose fore-parents were brought there as slaves" (Fossungu, 2015a: 80, original emphasis).

Marriage and Criminal Law Domains: Canadian Melting-Pot Formula versus American Unity-in-Diversity

Lawrence also stiffly brings out the folly in Canadian multiculturalism, crediting the USA with a real and sensible federal system. At the end of the day, Canada shares lots of deceptive features with West-Central Africa's Cameroon. As some critics have gone on to posit,

I usually cannot help laughing my lungs and jaws away when I hear people claiming *bijuralism* in Cameroon. When I read our colleagues of the other expression [French-speaking Cameroonians, that is], I keep wondering if they actually know what they are talking about when they conjure up this high-sounding *Droit Coutumier*. It just keeps recurring, especially as it would seem to have a whole caption and place reserved for it in *Juridis Périodique* (Fossungu, 1998: 4).

Similarly, one must have to laugh out lungs hearing that, marriage- and family-wise, Canada is multicultural while the U.S. is a melting-pot. The reverse seems to be the case as you will see in this discussion of sodomy. The formula for federalism and separation of powers would appear to be a real obstacle to the recognition of SSM in the United States. As explained by Miriam Smith,

focusing on the similarity of the same-sex marriage decisions in Canada and the U.S. obscures important differences in the relationship between courts and other political institutions in the two political systems. In the U.S., the separation of powers, the impact of federalism, and the access points provided by state-level initiatives have provided gay rights opponents with important levers to oppose the recognition of gay and lesbian rights. In contrast, in Canada, the opposition lacks these institutional levers (Smith, 2005: 226-27).

Margaret Gram Crehan's work provides the basis of many of these gay rights opponents; notably in Colorado where Focus on the Family is the primary anti-gay rights organization. Focus on the Family is a very large organization with a sophisticated direct marketing strategy, compared to the relatively small budgets of pro-SSM groups in the state (Crehan, 2013: 70). But this is not all that would hinder the lesbian and gay rights movements. To understand the American situation, an exploration of the Canadian formula is useful, especially in grasping why the U.S. is polarized and divided on the issue. This relates particularly to domains to which marriage and criminal law belong. Despite their similarities, there are profound differences in public policy outcomes between these two countries. Miriam Smith quotes Barry Adam who remarks that "legislation to bring gay and lesbian Americans full citizenship rights has been proceeding at a glacial pace," a situation Adam characterizes as yet another form of American exceptionalism (Smith, 2005: 225).

An important query that Miriam Smith poses is: What explains the public policy differences in human rights protections between the otherwise similar systems of Canada and the United States? An appropriate answer to the question belies all the incomprehension about what is going on in the U.S. regarding the SSM question. As Smith explains it off, Canada's 1969 law reforms, which legalized sodomy, formed a critical juncture in comparison with the failure of U.S. states to decriminalize sodomy. The legalization of sodomy has been the most important public policy issue in the lesbian and gay rights area in the U.S. over the last 20 years, whereas in Canada, sodomy laws are a non-issue. How this was done is quite interesting in view of variations in the practice of federalism (as to more of which, see Fossungu, 2013a: chapter 1), and I would let Smith better explain it expansively to you.

This difference between the policies of the two countries attracted little attention at the time; the change to Canadian law was made as part of a package of family law reforms designed on the British model of family law reform. The intent of the changes was to modernize family law; at the time the legalization of homosexual behavior (sodomy) attracted less public attention than other features of the reform package such as the easing of access to divorce. Several features of the institutional environment facilitated this critically important change in Canadian policy. First, unlike in the U.S., the federal division of powers in Canada allocates criminal law powers to the federal government. Second, the parliamentary system makes it much easier for a determined executive to pass its legislative agenda unopposed. In the U.S., the division of powers system provides more points of access for determined opponents and the criminal law regulation of sodomy is a power belonging to the states, not to the federal government. These differences have greatly exacerbated the difficulty of legalizing sodomy in the U.S. (Smith, 2005: 226)

These are very important issues that Crehan didn't have or ignored in her comparative study of three American states, and which could have conveniently answered her numerous questions posed on SSM, some of which are in earlier portions of this book. Miriam Smith's incisive comparative study not only resolves in a very convincing and authoritative way the query as to why homosexuals in the U.S. are finding it hard to have and enjoy equal citizenship rights,[52] but also

_____

[52] "This critical juncture in the evolution of public policies toward lesbians and gays," Smith writes, "has had important repercussions

disproves an earlier assertion that the Canadian courts (through decisions like *Re Same-Sex Marriages* of 2004) actually led the legislature in the matter of legalizing lesbian and gay rights. But it is not really like Crehan was unaware of the situation in Canada. It could just be that the American federal style is preferred for the innovation and other opportunities for better local rights protection, which seems to be absent in Canada. The division in America over the issue is loudly recognised. Nonetheless, Crehan argues,

> the diverse handling of same-sex marriage by the three states I studied, supports Brandeis' original vision of Federalism, for states to act as laboratories for social experiments. Whether choosing to pass a Defense of Marriage Amendment that leaves open the possibility for civil unions in Colorado; providing same-sex marriage rights via a judicial determination in Massachusetts; or utilizing the petition process to overturn same-sex marriage rights in California [and Hawaii], each state has determined their own course of action on this issue (Crehan, 2013: 153).

This can sort of give us an idea why *innovation* is such an unknown thing in Canada. It also explains why province to province variation in Canada has been less significant than state to state variation in the U.S. This is rather ironic, considering that the federal formula is adopted, in the first place, precisely to maintain unity in diversity rather a melting-

---

through policy debates on lesbian and gay rights. First, the lesbian and gay movement in the U.S. must counter the categorization of homosexuals as putative or potential criminals. This puts the movement in a much more defensive posture than the Canadian movement, which has not had to counter the stigma of criminalization" (Smith, 2005: 226).

pot position on issues like these. I would rather go for the American version of federalism than the Canadian deceptive Macdonaldian centralization (see Fossungu, 2013b: 95). Could this 'melting-potism' not be the rationale or force behind Quebec separatism, for instance? Explaining the need for the entrenchment of rights, John D. Whyte describes scenarios including

> one in which the fear and distaste by the majority for certain people [which] leads to the oppression of those people. The Canadian historical record reveals a number of instances of political passion directed against conspicuous minorities – Japanese Canadians, Hutterites, Doukhobors, [A]boriginal peoples, Jehovah's Witnesses, the Acadians, Metis, Roman Catholics, communists and separatists. All of these groups have, at some point, been seen as producing more social disruption and risk than society has been able to bear and all these groups have been governmentally burdened in order to reduce the fear that has surrounded their presence. In all of these cases the governmental assessment of risk has been facile and overstated. In all of these cases the governmental response has been more than merely disadvantageous to members of these groups. It has been brutal, community crushing, and life destroying. Political passion that is generated by the fear that there are communities whose practices subvert the fabric of our society is powerful and terrifying (Whyte, 1992: 473).

Much more importantly, in other words, why would the *Copyocracy* reject copying this time from federal USA, preferring copycatting unitary UK instead? Corbett may, after all, not be wrong in describing the Loyalists the way he does: 'conservatives dedicated to the pursuit of POGG in the style of English parliamentary democracy' (cited in Fossungu, 2013a: 148). The Swiss intriguing Territorial Bilingualism has clearly not resulted in the country splitting, the reverse instead being the rule. The never-ending conservatism and the diehard desire to dominate minorities in Canada would seem to be behind the override clause of the charter, legislation that, contrary to some sloppy idealization, was not made in heaven. I will thus instead go along with Bash who argues that the move towards a national solution for defending marriage is misplaced, pointing out how and why federalist principles are advantageous:

This federalist structure of joint sovereigns preserves to the people numerous advantages. It assures a decentralized government that will be more sensitive to the diverse needs of a heterogeneous society; it increases opportunity for citizen involvement in democratic processes; it allows for more innovation and experimentation in government; and it makes government more responsive by putting the States in competition for a mobile citizenry (cited in Crehan, 2013: 152).

Hollingsworth and *Windsor:* Giving Back States' Marriage Sovereignty?

One sees this fine thesis being validated in the two SSM cases from California and New York that came before the American Supreme Court. How all these 'controversial' court rulings would affect the conservatives' definition of marriage and the questions of federalism and of separation of powers, are problems that are addressed in this section. The section surveys the questions of federalism and separation of powers raised by the same-sex marriage court battles. The DOMA "has come before the U.S. Supreme Court, raising issues of federalism and separation of powers" (Crehan, 2013: 13). We have seen above that the case that was evidently behind the federal DOMA is *Baehr v. Lewin* (1993) in which Hawaii's Supreme Court ruled in favour of same-sex marriage. The federalism question was also raised in *Baker v. Nelson* and is very crucial because, although regulation of marriage has traditionally been left up to the states, the federal government in 1996 responded to state court decisions favourable to same-sex marriage by going ahead and passing the DOMA, which defines marriage as heterosexual monogamy. This came as "both state and federal legislatures believed they were under judicial assault from state courts" (Crehan, 2013: 18). This section looks at the *Hollingsworth* case from California and the *Windsor* one from New York that came before the Supreme Court, touching directly on federalism and separation of powers.

In July 2013 the U.S. Supreme Court issued rulings in both cases, *Windsor v. United States* and *Hollingsworth v. Perry.* These decisions were hailed as victories for proponents of same-sex marriage and both were considered to bolster state sovereignty. In *Hollingsworth,* the Court ruled that because California State officials had declined to appeal the trial court's decision against them, the proponents of Prop 8, who were appealing the decision, were not the proper party before the Court. The Court therefore was unable to issue a ruling, and instead sent the case back to the Trial Court, which had previously ruled that Prop 8 was unconstitutional. This has meant that same-sex marriage is once again legal in California. Some see the success by proponents of SSM in both cases before the U.S. Supreme Court as being tied to the distaste for federal involvement in marriage, considered by many to be a state issue.

Federalism relates both to the limits on the federal government in areas traditionally left or reserved to the states expressed by the Tenth Amendment to the U.S. Constitution and the ability of states to set their own laws and policies on such matters as marriage. The Tenth Amendment does not specifically outline what areas should be left up to state regulation but family law, including marriage, has traditionally been considered one such arena (Crehan, 2013: 151). On July 1, 2013, Susan Page of *USA Today*, commenting on the *Hollingsworth* and *Windsor* decisions, stated: "The court's decisions that opened the door to gay marriage in California and struck down a law that barred federal benefits for same-sex couples may well have boosted support in a country that was already moving in favor of same-sex marriage" (Page, 2013).

The issue in *Windsor* had to do with whether Section 3 of the DOMA, which defines the term "marriage" for all purposes under federal law as "only a legal union between one man and one woman as husband and wife," deprives same-sex couples who are lawfully married under the laws of their states (such as New York[53]) of the equal protection of the laws, as guaranteed by the Fifth Amendment to the Constitution of the United States. The U.S. Supreme Court struck down Section 3 of the DOMA as unconstitutional under the Equal Protection clause of the Fifth Amendment,

---

[53] For extensive discussion of New York's SSM legalization, see David Wexelblat, "Trojan Horse or Much Ado About Nothing? Analyzing the Religious Exemptions in New York's Marriage Equality Act" 20(4) *Journal of Gender, Social Policy & the Law* (2012), 961-993.

noting that the definition and regulation of marriage has traditionally fallen under the purview of the states.

Chapter 6

Findings and Conclusion

Recent statements made by the French political heavyweight Jacques Chiraq, who said that France does not have to be a benefactor, it must merely stop usurping Africa, are indicating a potential for change. Chiraq stated that failure to change French-African relations can have catastrophic consequences. 2012 Presidential candidate Jean Luc Mélenon stated that the CFA represents the severe mistake not to tie the western African economies to the economies of the European Union. Mélenon demanded that France abandons its veto right at the Boards of the African Central Banks (Lehmann, 2007).

This book set out to investigate the way in which the United States courts have handled the almost intractable issues generated by the tussle between the forces for legalizing SSM and those for banning it. The political role of courts in the United States has long puzzled non-Americans, especially those from continental Europe. A clear case is Alexis De Tocqueville from France. The struggle over SSM has squarely brought that role under critical scrutiny, pitching those who support a more activist judiciary against those calling for restraint. Judicial review is what the whole argument is about. Judicial review is the power to invalidate acts of legislators and executives. It is the most important and continuing relationship that a court can have with other political institutions (Waltman, 1988: 5). As the book has shown, constitutions merely express the "positivization" of higher values and judicial review is the method of rendering these values effective (Cappelletti, 1971: vii & x).

The scope of judicial review makes the Supreme Court of any country a centre of political power (Coomaraswamy, 1987: 2). It is noted that the U.S. courts enjoyed all these attributes, especially after Chief Justice Marshall's ruling in *Marbury* in 1803. As divisive as the SSM issue is, the United States courts have been able to navigate through it with a lot of carefully thought out rulings that laid down easy to predict paths for subsequent litigation. Litigation in this area, like that on abortion, is heavily charged with questions of morality or religion and no matter the direction of the courts' rulings some of the disputants would always find fault with the process. The question that may be asked concerns whether those who challenge the court as consisting of unelected officials would still make such claims if the court's ruling went their way.

The book has made some interesting findings not only in the out-of-court family politics but also relating to SSM litigation. In regard of family politics outside the courts, the temptation here is for me to entirely leave the discoveries to readers' assessment since these could be so many and diverse – depending on the family issues and type of family involved. These, in themselves, are so numerous. But if there is one trend or thesis that cuts across all of them, it is the remarkable absence of straightforwardness, highly clothed by deception (intentional and inadvertent) – hence, justifying 'Family Deception' in the title of this book. This finding thus makes it extremely hard for truthful persons involved in these relationships to succeed in doing whatever it is, no matter how much they try. In other words, "perpetual liars must obviously be thinking always that everyone else is lying to them, making it extremely hard for the truthful to ever succeed in doing anything with them on board, no matter how much one tries" (Fossungu, 2015a: 70).

On litigation, the purely African side is zero. That the issue is nonsensical in most of Africa is easily laid to rest by the following assertion:

Why shouldn't stealing become a national trait in Zaire when Number One Zairian does that bidding? Didn't embezzlement also become a national government style in Cameroon when Paul Biya asked a journalist who was pointing accusing fingers at a minister: "*Est-ce que vous avez des preuves?*" Of course, we need proof for every accusation. But is it not for the courts to demand for that evidence? What does the Cameroon president actually mean then? That he is judge and player, for sure. That could also explain why he alone can decide when to put any of his stealing/embezzling 'collaborators' behind bars any time and any how without any court or person asking for proof: since he always has a 'stealing dossier' on all these so-called collaborators" (Fossungu, 2015a: 108)

On the NNA side, the following findings are noted. The U.S. courts have been found to be more suited to ably respond to changing public opinion in regard of SSM than the other branches of government. We have seen this trend in state court decisions like *Baehr v. Lewin* (1993) and *Goodridge v. Massachusetts Department of Health* (2003). On the other hand, the other branches have reacted to court rulings by rushing to pass DOMA that seeks to maintain the traditional sectarian meaning of marriage. At the federal or national level, *Lawrence v. Texas* (2003) represents the Supreme Court's moving with the changing public opinion by overturning its own earlier ruling on the constitutionality of states' sodomy laws.

The second finding has to do with courts' flexibility in defining the concept of marriage. In 2003 they moved away from the procreation idea of marriage (as stressed in *Baker v. Nelson* (1971), *Morrison v. Sadler*, and *James v. Hallahan*) to regarding it as a civil institution in *Goodridge* (2003). Third, with the *Lawrence v. Texas* ruling that shattered the criminality of sodomy, it is hard to see why SSM would continue to stay out of legalization. The fourth finding concerns the federalism face of SSM in the United States, issues that seem to have been laid to rest by both *Hollingsworth v. Perry* (2013) and *Windsor v. United States* (2013). One should note as well that the failure of the FMA to pass in the Senate probably had federalism concerns tied to it.

It is true that the American system makes it harder than in Canada for homosexuals to attain equality in marriage rights across the country. It is also true to say that no society is homogenous in its values, not even Canada where not everyone is in support of or against certain values, including same-sex unions. Even in the LGBT community there is discord. American gay activists have long squabbled over their ultimate goal: is it liberty or equality? Do gays seek the freedom to live the lives they desire—or do gays seek the respect from straight people that is the prerequisite for them to invite LGBTs into society as fellow citizens? Some do not see liberty and equality as being at cross-purposes, and many policies sought by LGBT activists can be rightly said to promote both goals. But in their ideal types, some experts believe that liberty and equality imply quite different self-conceptions for LGBT people vis-à-vis society and the state (Egan and Sherrill, 2005: 229). To be sure, the Supreme Court in *Lawrence* struck down criminal statutes based upon a moral distinction between heterosexual and homosexual conduct. But senators considering the FMA had every right to interpret the Constitution as they see fit and to not feel bound by the Court when amending the Constitution. Commentators think that with the FMA, conservatives had an opportunity to counter the increasing acceptance of homosexual conduct and limit what some believed were the implications of the Court's opinion in *Lawrence* (Liu and Sherrill, 2005: 213).

Some critics would believe the Canadian SSM situation is more advanced than the American. But I am not sure about that because the U.S. courts appear to be better at the job. It is indisputable, however, that no system of judicial review is perfect, making the pursuit of a fool-proof solution in this matter a futile exercise. The only way we can achieve such a system would perhaps be to have our judges come from some other planet than earth: which, by the way, would not still have clothed us with a perfect system since these unearthly judges would hardly, if not *never*, be able to understand how earthlings operate. Perhaps we should just be happy that our judges in northern North America have both the independence from the other branches and the power to be able to strike down unconstitutional laws; attributes that many of their counterparts elsewhere do not enjoy. Secondly, that these judges are not entirely 'free agents' in their decision-making. Their decisions are never entirely, and seldom are they radically disconnected from mainstream values. On the whole, American Courts appear to have dabbled well with the intricate litigation between the SSM legalization drive and the religious traditionalists, moving boldly along with the changing times.

References

Akokpari, John K. (2001) "Globalisation and the Challenges for the African State" *Nordic Journal of African Studies* 10:2: 188-209.

Benson, Peter and Dorothy Williams (2011) "Religion on Capitol Hill: Myths and Realities (1982)" in Amy E. Black, Douglas L. Koopman, and Larycia A. Hawkins (eds.) *Religion and American Politics: Classical and Contemporary Perspectives* (New York: Longman), 274-278.

Bentele, Keith Gunnar, Rebecca Sager, Sarah A. Soule, and Gary Adler, Jr. (2014) "Breaking Down the Wall between Church and State: State Adoption of Religious Inclusion Legislation, 1995–2009" *Journal of Church and State* 56:3: 503-533.

Black, Amy E., Douglas L. Koopman, and Larycia A. Hawkins (eds.) (2011) *Religion and American Politics: Classical and Contemporary Perspectives* (New York: Longman).

Bogart, W.A. (1994) *Courts and Country: The Limits of Litigation and the Social and Political Life in Canada* (Toronto: Oxford University Press).

Buckley, Thomas (2011) "A Mandate for Anti-Catholicism: The Blaine Amendment (2004)" in Black, Amy E., Douglas L. Koopman, and Larycia A. Hawkins (eds.) *Religion and American Politics: Classical and Contemporary Perspectives* (New York: Longman), 321-324.

Campbell, David E. and Robert D. Putnam (2012) "God and Caesar in America: Why Mixing Religion and Politics Is Bad for Both" *Foreign Affairs* 91:2: 34-43.

Cappelletti, M. (1971) *Judicial Review in the Contemporary World* (New York: The Bobbs-Merrill Company Inc.).

Coomaraswamy, R. (1987) "Towards an Engaged Judiciary" in N. Tiruchelvam and R. Coomaraswamy (eds.) *The Role of the Judiciary in Plural Societies* (New York: St. Martin's Press), 1.

Crehan, Margaret Gram (2013) *The Divided States of America: A Comparative Case Study of Same-Sex Marriage in the United States* (Ph.D. Dissertation, Northeastern University).

Cunningham, Maurice T. (2005) "Catholics and the ConCon: The Church's Response to the Massachusetts Gay Marriage Decision" *Journal of Church and State* 47:1: 19-42.

Dickson, Brian (1992) "The Democratic Character of the Charter of Rights" in F.L. Morton (ed.) *Law, Politics and the Judicial Process in Canada* (2nd edition) (Calgary: University of Calgary Press), 464-466.

Dimond, P.R. (1989) *The Supreme Court and Judicial Choice: The Role of Provisional Review in a Democracy* (Ann Arbor: The University of Michigan Press).

Egan, Patrick J. and Kenneth Sherrill (2005) "Marriage and the Shifting Priorities of a New Generation of Lesbians and Gays" *Political Science and Politics* 38:2: 229-232.

Fossungu, Peter Ateh-Afac (2015a) *Africans and Negative Competition in Canadian Factories: Revamping Canada's Immigration, Employment and Welfare Policies?* (Bamenda: Langaa RPCIG).

_____ (2015b) *The HISOFE Dictionary of Midnight Politics: Expibasketical Theories on Afrikentication and African Unity* (Bamenda: Langaa RPCIG).

_____ (2014) *Africa's Anthropological Dictionary on Love and Understanding: Marriage and the Tensions of Belonging in Cameroon* (Bamenda, Cameroon: Langaa RPCIG).

_____ (2013a) *Understanding Confusion in Africa: The Politics of Multiculturalism and Nation-building in Cameroon* (Bamenda, Cameroon: Langaa RPCIG).

_____ (2013b) *Democracy and Human Rights in Africa: The Politics of Collective Participation and Governance in Cameroon* (Bamenda, Cameroon: Langaa RPCIG).

_____ (2013c) *Africans in Canada: Blending Canadian and African Lifestyles?* (Bamenda, Cameroon: Langaa RPCIG).

_____ (1998) "Confused Cameroon Law" *The Herald* N° 659 (11-13 September), 4.

Gerstmann, Evan (2005) "Litigating Same-Sex Marriage: Might the Courts Actually Be Bastions of Rationality?" *Political Science and Politics* 38:2: 217-220.

Golomb, B. (1973) "Selection of the Judiciary: For Election" in G.R. Winters, ed. *Judicial Selection and Tenure* (Chicago: The American Judicature Society), 74.

Haider-Markel, Donald P. and Mark R. Joslyn (2005) "Attribution and the Regulation of Marriage: Considering the Parallels Between Race and Homosexuality" *Political Science and Politics* 38:2: 233-239.

Hillygus, D. Sunshine and Todd G. Shields (2005) "Moral Issues and Voter Decision Making in the 2004 Presidential Election" *Political Science and Politics* 38:2: 201-209.

How the Court Became Supreme, "John Marshall, Marbury v. Madison, and Judicial Review—How the Court Became Supreme" available @ http://edsitement.neh.gov/lesson-plan/john-marshall-marbury-v-madison-and-judical-review-how-court-became-supreme [accessed in November 2014].

Irons, Peter (2011) "A People's History of the Supreme Court: The Men and the Women Whose Cases and

Decisions Have Shaped our Constitution (2006)" in Black, Amy E., Douglas L. Koopman, and Larycia A. Hawkins (eds.) *Religion and American Politics: Classical and Contemporary Perspectives* (New York: Longman), 328-331.

James, Harold (2009) *The Creation and Destruction of Value: The Globalization Cycle* (Cambridge, Mass.: Harvard University Press).

Kincaid, John (2014) "Is Federalism Still the 'Dark Continent' of Political Science Teaching? Yes and No" *Political Science and Politics* 47:4: 877-883.

Lehmann, Christof (2007) "French Africa Policy Damages African and European Economies:" @ nsnbc.me/2012/10/12/french-africa-policy-damages-african-and.

Lewis, Gregory B. (2005) "Same-Sex Marriage and the 2004 Presidential Election" *Political Science and Politics* 38:2: 195-199.

Linker, Damon (2015) "God's Banker by Gerald Posner" @ http://www.langaa-rpcig.net/+God-s-Bankers-by-Gerald-Posner+.html

Liu, Frederick and Stephen Macedo (2005) "The Federal Marriage Amendment and the Strange Evolution of the Conservative Case against Gay Marriage" *Political Science and Politics* 38:2: 211-215.

Lublin, David (2005) "The Strengthening of Party and Decline of Religion in Explaining Congressional Voting Behavior on Gay and Lesbian Issues" *Political Science and Politics* 38:2: 241-245.

Morton, F.L. (1992) *Law, Politics and the Judicial Process in Canada* (2nd edition) (Calgary: University of Calgary Press).

Oldmixon, Elizabeth Anne (2011) "Uncompromising Positions: God, Sex, and the U.S. House of

Representatives (2005)" in Amy E. Black, Douglas L. Koopman, and Larycia A. Hawkins (eds.) *Religion and American Politics: Classical and Contemporary Perspectives* (New York: Longman), 285-289.

Page, Susan (2013) "Poll: Support for gay marriage hits high after ruling" available @ http://www.usatoday.com/story/news/politics/2013/07 /01/poll-supreme-court-gay-marriage-affirmative-action-voting-rights/2479541/ (accessed on November 27, 2014).

Patrikios, Stratos (2008) "American Republican Religion? Disentangling the Causal Link between Religion and Politics in the US" *Political Behavior* 30: 367-389.

Putnam, Robert, and David Campbell (2012) *American Grace: How Religion Divides and Unites Us* (New York: Simon & Schuster).

Radamaker, Dallis (1988) "The Courts in France" in Jerold L. Waltman and Kenneth M. Holland (eds.) *The Political Role of Law Courts in Modern Democracies* (New York: St. Martin's Press), 129-152.

Riggle, Ellen D.B., Jerry D. Thomas and Sharon S. Rostosky (2005) "The Marriage Debate and Minority Stress" *Political Science and Politics* 38:2: 221-224.

Russell, Peter H. (1992) "Standing Up for Notwithstanding" in F.L. Morton (ed.) *Law, Politics and the Judicial Process in Canada* (2nd edition) (Calgary: University of Calgary Press), 474-485.

Smiley, Donald (1992) "Courts, Legislatures, and the Protection of Human Rights" in F.L. Morton (ed.) *Law, Politics and the Judicial Process in Canada* (2nd edition) (Calgary: University of Calgary Press), 462-464.

Smidt, Corwin (2011) "Making Sense of the American Religious Landscape" in Amy E. Black, Douglas L. Koopman, and Larycia A. Hawkins (eds.) *Religion and American Politics: Classical and Contemporary Perspectives* (New York: Longman), 106-113.

Smith, Miriam (2005) "The Politics of Same-Sex Marriage in Canada and the United States" *Political Science & Politics* 38:2: 225-228.

Theriault, Sean M. and Herscher F. Thomas III (2014) "The Diffusion of Support for Same-Sex Marriage in the US Senate" *Political Science and Politics* 47:4: 824-828.

Thoreson, Ryan (2013) "Beyond Equality: The Post-Apartheid Counternarrative of Trans and Intersex Movements in South Africa" *African Affairs* 112:449: 646-665.

Tweed, Thomas A. (1992) "An American Pioneer in the Study of Religion: Hannah Adams (1755-1831) and Her *Dictionary of All Religions*" *Journal of the American Academy of Religion* LX/3: 437-464.

Wahlbeck, Paul (2011) "Judicial Decision Making and Religion Cases" in Amy E. Black, Douglas L. Koopman, and Larycia A. Hawkins (eds.) *Religion and American Politics: Classical and Contemporary Perspectives* (New York: Longman), 313-321.

Waltman, Jerold L. "Introduction" in Jerold L. Waltman and Kenneth M. Holland, eds., *The Political Role of Law Courts in Modern Democracies* (New York: St. Martin's Press, 1989), 1-5.

Wenzel, Nikolai G. (2013), "Judicial Review and Constitutional Maintenance: John Marshall, Hans Kelsen, and the Popular Will" *Political Science and Politics* 46:3: 591-598.

Westbrook, Neil P. (2010) *The Institution of Marriage and the Role of the Local Church: A Study at Neel Road Baptist Church in Salisbury, North Carolina* (Ph.D. Dissertation, McAfee School of Theology, Atlanta, Georgia).

Whyte, John D. (1992) "On Not Standing for Notwithstanding" in F.L. Morton (ed.) *Law, Politics and the Judicial Process in Canada* (2nd edition) (Calgary: University of Calgary Press), 467-474.

Wuerl, Donald Cardinal (2015) "Silencing the Church's Voice" Cardinal Wuerl's e-letter@adw.org (of the Archdiocese of Washington Office of Digital Media) sent out on March 2, 2015, as posted by Oben Besong on SobaAmerica Forum on March 2, 2015 at 9.45 PM.

Yancy, George (2015) "Noam Chomsky on the Roots of American Racism" @ http://mobile.nytimes.com/blogs/opinionator/2015/03/18/noam-chomsky-on-the-roots-of-american-racism/